Excel 2022

From Beginner to Expert | The Ultimate Guide to Master the Essential Functions and Formulas in Less Than 10 Minutes per Day With Step-by-Step Tutorials and Practical Examples.

D1521817

CONTENTS

INTRODUCTION

Excel is a powerful spreadsheet application from Microsoft. It's been around for over 30 years and has evolved from a simple calculator to a comprehensive tool for financial analysis, business intelligence, and data visualization. The newest version of Excel is presented in this book with information about its most exciting new features.

Even if you're already familiar with the previous versions of Microsoft Excel, this book provides a great beginning point for getting up to speed on the new features. The goal is to give you the information you need to do your job more efficiently. You can then explore the new features in greater depth at your own pace.

It's an exciting time for Excel users, with Microsoft continuing its tradition of offering free upgrades with each new release of Excel. The best way to upgrade is by installing the Office 365 application on your computer. Linking your Microsoft account with Office 365 lets you download and install updates seamlessly. It also gives you access to all the latest features added to Office 365 like docs.com, One Drive for Business, and Skype for Business. Microsoft is adding new features over time, but these features are only half the story over the long term. The other half is how you and your team can use them. Best of all, you don't need any special skills or training - - just an existing knowledge of Excel that you can extend through these new resources. Just as important as new features are improvements in Excel's usability and security. These improvements allow you to work faster and be more accurate at the same time.

LIST BUSINESS CASES WHERE EXCEL IS USED

Spreadsheets are helpful for so many different tasks. They can be used to analyze data, calculate results, or even provide feedback information. To accomplish these tasks, users of Excel have developed dozens of ways to use this tool. These ways are not always mutually exclusive. For example, you might use one method on Monday and another on Tuesday for the same task. You can see just how many different uses of excel there are by looking at the "User stories" section below.

Excel is a universal tool that can be used in several business cases. Below you will find some of the most common ones:

1. To simplify complex processes in areas such as financial analysis, sales forecasting, and budgeting.
2. To facilitate everyday tasks in various professions such as inventory control, human resources management, and product development planning.
3. To streamline tedious operations such as data entry and manual calculations.
4. To easily present data in report form in government, education, and health care.
5. To create advanced graphics in business intelligence, engineering, and scientific research.
6. To create 2D and 3D visualizations of data presented to stakeholders for decision-making in geology, meteorology, and astronomy.
7. To manage and track data in areas such as business intelligence and health care.
8. To analyze and control costs in inventory management, capital budgeting, and purchasing.
9. To provide feedback on products in product design, marketing, and quality assurance.

10. To create dashboards in areas such as operating information, engineering, and human resources management.

Everyone from project managers to entry-level employees has access to computers and electronic devices in today's office environment. In return for the convenience, you must expect specific security measures, including malware protection through antivirus software or a firewall. Microsoft Excel is no exception.

There is no failing of ways to use Excel for business purposes. If you're new to the tool, the sheer number of uses can be overwhelming. But don't be daunted -- take it one step at a time. This book provides an overview that will get you started with some concrete work examples. Once you get past the initial learning curve, you'll discover how easy it is to create Excel spreadsheets and charts on your own. Remember, anyone can be an Excel user if they know the right way to do it.

Chapter 1.   WHEN SHOULD YOU USE EXCEL?

There are different situations when it's best to use Excel:

- Financial Reports
- Sales Reports
- Inventory Management

Each of these examples has one thing in common: tracking data over time. It can often be challenging to track your sales over a year if you're running a business. Or maybe you would like to know how much money you've made from your inventory to better predict future needs. Excel is perfect for these sorts of tasks.

One of the most important things to remember about Excel is that it is not a one-size-fits-all tool. If you're not comfortable with the software, then the chances are good that you'll be spending most of your time frustrated instead of working effectively. The goal should always be to find the tool that works best for managing your schedule and the data you're working with.

It's essential to have a more comprehensive understanding of Excel to administer work efficiently. There are different techniques to improve your efficiency, but it's usually best to start on the more accessible end of the spectrum first. By mastering those techniques and learning about how Excel works, you'll soon be able to take on more complex tasks with ease.

Using Excel can be a great time-saver, but it's up to you whether it's worth your time. Keep in mind that the most significant issues regarding work efficiency are due to a lack of knowledge about Excel. In most cases, it's better to start on the more accessible end of the spectrum before moving on to more complex tasks. Improving your efficiency will allow you to complete more tasks in less time. It'll also eliminate the need to worry about procrastinating while you're working on something important.

Many people try to tackle too many things at once and end up spending most of their time getting distracted by other projects. If you break your tasks into separate parts, it'll be much easier for you to stay focused and get everything done within a reasonable amount of time. This is another example of how working with Excel can improve your efficiency.

When you're working on a large project, there's a good chance that it'll require several different Excel spreadsheets to be created. When dealing with multiple spreadsheets, you'll want to make sure they're all using the same data in each of them. This will provide you a better idea of what's going on with your projects throughout the day.

It's also essential to use Excel for tracking data over time for projects. These tasks can be complicated to work with when you're not familiar with Excel. The software can handle these types of projects with ease, so it's up to you whether it coheres for your business.

When working on a spreadsheet, it's crucial that you understand how Excel works. There is a lot of trial and error involved when figuring out how the program works, but once you take the time to get going, it'll be easy to handle everything efficiently. It's essential to spend a little time learning how Excel works before using it for your work.

The first step is to learn how the program works by exploring its different features. Then, you can create a spreadsheet that has all your products listed on it. As you make each invoice, you'll need to keep this spreadsheet updated with the latest information. Then, you might have another sheet that has all your products listed in it again, but this time it includes their current inventory level. You'll also want to create a report that calculates the difference between these two numbers. Similarly, if you always work with the same data in every spreadsheet throughout your project, everything should fall into place once you're done.

Chapter 2. 7 THINGS YOU SHOULD KNOW ABOUT MICROSOFT EXCEL

Many people think Excel is just for mathematicians and accounting professionals. Still, the truth is that this versatile spreadsheet application has grown to be a must-have tool for graphic designers, educators, and even writers. Whether you're an expert with Excel or a novice, not having a good skill level in this program can prevent you from advancing your career. And sometimes, even if you have some experience in Excel, the very nature of the program can be challenging to master. So here are 7 things every excel user should know about mastering this versatile software. If you're ready to take your skills with Excel beyond the beginner level, read on.

CUSTOMIZE YOUR MOUSE

The speediest and easiest way to get more out of Excel is to set up your mouse for Excel navigation. Click the View tab and then click Customize Quick Access Toolbar on the ribbon. In the Choose Commands From the dropdown, select Commands Not in the Ribbon.

Find and select "Grid" in the list by clicking on it once and then clicking Add.

INPUT DATA ON SCREEN

Having your spreadsheet onscreen is convenient, but it can also be distracting. To avoid interrupting your work, keep your data in a separate document – like a spreadsheet. Then, whenever you're working in Excel, simply open the paper instead of the spreadsheet and make changes from there.

MASTER NUMBERS IN EXCEL

If you're new to Excel, learning how to use numbers can seem like a daunting task. But don't beat yourself up. Excel's new user interface makes it easier to enter and edit numbers than ever.

First, activate the navigation pane by clicking on the View tab > Show View Options dropdown > Navigation Pane checkbox. Then, click on "Number" in the left column to open a number grid in Excel that lets you input numbers and formulas as if you were using a calculator.

CREATE A DROP DOWN LIST

One of Excel's most useful features is its ability to sort and analyze data. But sorting and analyzing data can be a hassle if you must do it manually. If you have a drop-down list typed over, highlight the entire list and then click on the Data tab > Validation. From there, click on "allow" beside all listed items except your drop-down menu item, which should read "list."

CREATE FORMULAS ON THE FLY

Formulas are a big reason many people shy away from Excel, but formulas can be straightforward – even if you're new to spreadsheets. Instead of retyping the formulas, you need repeatedly, type the formula once but press Alt+Shift+Enter. This will produce the formula on every row as required.

LEARN TO USE THE COMMAND BUTTON

The easiest way to learn more about Excel is to use formula columns. By default, when you enter data into a column, the program will try to calculate a value and present that as a result. But with a simple 2-click process, you can change those columns into "user input" columns that let you opt-in or out of the automatic calculation.

ANALYZE YOUR SPREADSHEET

One of the most significant limitations of spreadsheets is that you can only analyze and evaluate your work when you're in Excel, but what if you could explore your spreadsheet without opening it? That's precisely what the VLookup function is for.

Like the SUM function, VLookup automatically charts your data when you use it and produces an output table that collates all results. In addition, you can "group" statistics by different criteria – even if your data doesn't follow a normal distribution. For example, you can put all the sales figures in column B but gather all the sales figures by product in column C – even though they're not both related to product prices.

One of the most repeated misconceptions people have about Excel is that it can only analyze numerical data. It's an excellent tool for analyzing almost any data or process – whether you're calculating sales figures or tracking your weekly weight loss.

The Microsoft Excel 2019 user interface is intuitive and robust – giving you unprecedented control over the data in your spreadsheet, regardless of your skill level.

So next time you're ready to figure out how to use Excel, keep those tips in mind!

Chapter 3.   EXCEL'S ADVANCED FEATURES AND FUNCTIONS

Excel is an advantageous and versatile spreadsheet application used for many purposes. However, like any application, Excel has certain features that are not always obvious but can make the user experience more efficient. Below we'll look at some of these lesser-known features and see what benefits they provide:

THE FILL HANDLE

This feature will allow you to easily copy the value from one cell to another nearby partition. For your convenience, the fill handle is located on either side of the fill handle button on the bottom portion of the formula bar. This makes it very convenient to copy from one cell to a nearby cell without using the mouse quickly.

COPY FROM REFERENCE CELLS

If you are using references in your formula, you can copy a value from a reference cell and paste it into another cell by holding down the SHIFT key and clicking on the desired reference cell.

CLIPBOARD VIEWER

You can quickly see what is currently on the clipboard by holding down shift and clicking on the fill handle. The fill handle will change from a clipboard shape to a clipboard with a checkmark. This represents what is currently on the clipboard in your current workbook. If you want to paste something from your workbook, click on the checkmark, and away you go.

FORMULAS AND CALCULATIONS

In Excel, formulas are the backbone of everything. Formula is simply a string of text containing a set of numbers. This is one way Excel makes formulas easy to use and understand. You can use the F2 key to run a formula in the formula bar. However, if you want to see what your formula will look like when inserted into a cell, press on the cell that contains the formula and then select Formulas > Formulas and calculations.

MSGBOX

This feature allows you to quickly see what is on your clipboard by showing a message box containing whatever is currently on your clipboard. This is useful when you need to copy something, such as a web address, and do not want to make any other changes to your original copy. To use the MsgBox feature, all you must do is press F2 on your keyboard, type or paste the message or text you want to see in a message box and click on OK.

WRAP TEXT

This feature allows you to easily format text by wrapping it around another cell's text value. This is done by clicking on the cell you want the text to appear in, clicking on Home > Alignment, and clicking Wrap Text. You then highlight the cell you want to wrap text around, and lastly, type your text into the second cell.

VLOOKUP

The Vlookup function allows you to search for a specific value in one or many columns based on the values in other columns. This is useful when searching for a particular value based on the values in different columns. When searching for a bargain, you must give the VLOOKUP function at least two arguments. The first argument must be the column where you want to find the value, and the second argument is the column(s) that want to be searched. In return, VLOOKUP will return a number representing how many rows in that column(s) contain the exact value you specified in your first argument.

FILTER

The Filter feature allows you to search for a specific value based on more columns in an Excel spreadsheet. This is useful when searching in a particular matter in one or more columns in your spreadsheet. To use the filter feature, select the range you want to filter, and then go to Data > Filter. You will be enquired to select the one or more columns to be filtered. In return, Excel will search for your specified value in that column.

TRIM

The TRIM function allows you to remove any spaces from the beginning or end of a string of text. This is useful when you have data with spaces at the beginning or end of each cell and remove them. To use this function, highlight the cell you want to trim spaces from and click on Formulas > Trim. In your dialog box, type the exact name of the trim function you want to run.

Pivot table

Pivot tables allow you to quickly summarize large amounts of data without the need to do a lot of analysis. It is useful when you have lots of data that you need to summarize. To use the Pivot table, select the cell where you want your pivot table to appear and click on either Insert > Tables > PivotTable or go to Insert > Table, then click on PivotTable. Give it a name and, if needed, specify the range that it should use as its source data. After this is completed, you will be provided with a blank pivot table with fields listed along the top and data in columns below. You can then enter your data into this pivot table and see how it will summarize the data by looking at the fields along the top. To add more lots or see what the summarized data looks like, click on any of the fields along the top. These fields will then be added at the bottom, and your original data will be summarized in each column you selected for this pivot table.

Text to Columns

This method is an Excel version of what some call a "Conditional Formatting" method which requires Microsoft Access. This method allows you to apply formatting/colors/etc. To a column of cells based on a value in an adjacent cell. To use this method, highlight a cell containing the value you want to apply the condition to, then click on the Home > Conditional Formatting button. In this dialog box, all you must do is choose the format that should be applied and apply it where you want. For example, if you wanted to use a specific color for all the cells in the column that was highlighted, click on "Fill Color" in the upper right corner. In return, Excel will apply your color/format to all cells in the highlighted column based on your value.

Paste Special

The Paste Special feature is useful when you need to paste a cell's formatting or value but not its cell location. This is useful for copying values, but not the formulas that use those values. To use this feature, select the cells you want to copy. Next, highlight the cells where you want to paste those copied values and click on Home > Paste > Paste Special.

PASTE AS PICTURE

The Paste as Picture feature is useful when you want to paste values as pictures. This is handy when you want to paste an image of a formula but not its cell location. To use this feature, select the cells you want to copy. Next, highlight the cells where you want to paste those copied values and click on Home > Paste > Paste Special. Select "Paste as Picture" and click OK in the dialog box that appears.

RIBBON ICON FUNCTIONS

Although there is nothing wrong with the classic menu system that was found in previous versions of Excel, the Ribbon brings some features to the table that were previously unavailable. When you click on a Ribbon icon, it will expand to display additional commands and buttons. One of the best things about the Ribbon is that it provides fast access to various commands and tools.

These are just certain of the features in Excel that you should know how to use. There are many more features that you should learn that will make your time in Excel much more effortless. Continue reading this book to learn more.

Chapter 4.   5 WAYS TO MASTER EXCEL

If you're like me, you've probably had the sinking sensation that no matter how much time and energy you put into Excel – learning shortcuts, mastering formulas – there's always more to learn. And if we're being factual with each other, it cannot be very comforting. But as I remind myself every day: it's okay to be overwhelmed. Ask your friends for help. Ask your co-workers. Ask the person beside you on the train, or they're all desperate for Excel help too!

The exact approach you should take is beyond the scope of this book, and this book can offer some general suggestions for getting started. First, don't be discouraged by the steep learning curve or feel like you already know everything there is to know about Excel – there's always more to learn. However, if you want to jump into the deep end and master Excel there are a few essential things to keep in mind:

1. Don't get worried on trying to learn EVERYTHING. If you're starting, it's helpful to have a little bit of direction on what you should know first, and that's where this book comes in.

2. Watch for shortcuts and workarounds. Once you've got the basics down, start paying attention to the things that frustrate or confuse you. If there's a shortcut, find it! If there's a workaround, learn it! Before long, this will be your second nature and help you save time, effort, and frustration when running your Excel models.

3. Have patience. There's always more to learn. Mastering Excel is a long-term project, and it doesn't happen overnight. You'll improve with time and experience, just like any skill or art, but there are some things you can do to accelerate up the process. For example, if you're struggling with learning shortcuts on one formula, use that formula while others are running and write down the formulas you need to memorize next (or ask your co-workers for their suggestions).

4. Find time to practice and learn Excel every day. It's easy to get caught up in the daily grind and not have time to improve your Excel skills. However, if you schedule time every day – whether it's 15 or 30 minutes each day – you'll continue to improve your skills and be on your way to mastery. You could even try booking a specific time each week, like Sunday nights when you're less likely to make plans or a few times a month on evenings or weekends.

5. Don't be frightened to ask for guidance. When you're feeling frustrated about Excel, don't hesitate to ask your manager or co-workers for a few minutes to speak with them about where you're stuck and what they've found that helps. Or just Google the problem – if you don't want to talk about it in person, that's fine. Know someone else has already dealt with this issue successfully.

In the end, learning Excel can feel overwhelming and intimidating. It's also a long-term project – it takes time and experience to become a master, but there are some matters you can do to jump-start the process and speed up the learning curve: set a goal for what you want to learn first, watch for shortcuts, practice every day, and don't be intimidated to ask for help.

Chapter 5. EXCEL TIPS AND TRICKS

Excel has always been one of the best extraordinary influential pieces of software out there, but it can be intimidating for new users. It's no wonder people are often hesitant to even try it. If you're feeling overwhelmed by Excel's many features and functions, this chapter will empower you with everything you need to master the program.

EXCEL TIPS

- -Know how to create and use Pivot Tables, Filters, and VLOOKUP functions. These are advantageous Excel features when summarizing a large amount of data quickly and easily. - Know how to create charts and graphs with Excel. Most Excel users are familiar with essential charts, but excel has many more advanced types of charts, such as 3D pie charts, line graphs made up of polar axes and square root scale factor, Gantt chart, and stacked bar chart.

- Learn how to create an intelligent range on your spreadsheets by setting absolute reference ranges in your formulas. Brilliant ranges make it easier to enter data in multiple columns at once. For example, when you enter your sales data in several columns, you don't have to enter the sales figures for each column separately. You can enter all the data for one bottom row and then enter the sales for each top row. This will preserve a lot of time and trouble.

- Learn to work with worksheets in Excel by dividing your spreadsheet into several rows or columns and then selecting which cells you want to see on each worksheet.

- Know how to work on two spreadsheets at the same time.

- Learn how to use Excel's built-in AutoSum feature. This feature is great for calculating sums and sums for numbers in a preestablished range of cells. This can free you a lot of time when accounting, mainly when calculating profit margins and net worth.

- Learn the uses of Excel's built-in Mail Merge function, which lets you automatically send out documents such as letters and labels with personalized information already inserted.

Excel is one of the most popular programs in the office. However, even professional users often forget about some of its advanced features.

Here are some of the most advanced tricks that will take your Excel knowledge to the next level.

1. Track how much time it takes you to do specific tasks in one day with conditional formatting. If it takes less than 10 minutes, highlight the cells green. If it takes more than 10 minutes but less than 30 minutes, highlight them yellow, and if it gives you more than 30 minutes but less than 60 minutes, highlight them orange. This will give you a clear visual representation of how much time-specific tasks take you to do, and you can use your newfound knowledge to streamline your processes.

2. Use the pivot table and sort data. It's easy to see the average amount of time that something takes you to do. You can also filter the data by category or value to determine which task takes up the most of your time.

3. Sometimes, it is hard to find the value you are looking for if there are a lot of other values on the same row. Using the formula =VLOOKUP(), you can look up the value of a particular column at any given position in your data table.

4. If you have a massive table of data and you need to find the average for the entire table, instead of manually doing it, use this formula: =AVERAGEIF(some cell, C5:C8,")=. This will allow you to enter your average formula in one cell as an average and then use

conditional formatting, and it will highlight the cells that meet that condition. This way, you can change the numbers in your function without retyping them into every cell.

5. If you want a number with specific formatting within an Excel formula, you can use the "=" operator. For example, if you're going to display $100 but in a currency format in the spreadsheet, instead of using =",=Currency," you can set up the number format in the HOME option and select CURRENCY. This will display $100 within your document in the currency format that is specified.

6. When you have a large table of data and you want to filter specific columns using a drop-down list, it can be challenging to keep track of what column will apply each time. Using this formula is as easy as typing in a number between 1-7. This formula will filter through all the numbers in your table and check if they were used before. Then it will output the number that has been used before, making it very easy to find which value is being used from the list.

7. This formula is a variation of the "IFS" formula, which allows you to create conditional logic in Excel and compares two values based on a specified condition. The IF function is commonly used to compare two values logically. However, it will only work for single values or when you compare by less than, equal to, or greater than. To fix this, use a variation of the IFS formula. This will result in a more efficient procedure not encumbered by single values and logical comparisons.

8. A common problem many users have is selecting data from within a table. Often it is easy to choose the wrong cell because you don't know what cell you are choosing from. To fix this problem, you can use the FIND method. For example, if you have a table that is sorted by dates and you want to select the date for a particular cell,

use the formula =FIND(B4, "date"). This formula will select your date from within the table and put it into a cell.

9. It is often complicated to see what cells are highlighted in Excel. There are a few ways you can use to do this. The first way is using conditional formatting. Highlight the cells you want to see highlighted, and then select the "Conditional Formatting" option from the home tab that will let you to highlight specific cells based on certain formulas in your sheet. This will allow you to quickly scan your data and see which duplicated numbers.

10. Sometimes, it is necessary to perform extensive calculations in Excel, and it would take too long if you were to do them manually. You can use the "SUMIF()" formula in Excel to do this. This formula is used to sum up, cells based on specific criteria. This will allow you to enter multiple formulas with the same function, and Excel will combine them into one formula and perform the task for you instantly.

Now, you got the tips and tricks that will take your Excel knowledge to the next level and will help you improve your workplace efficiency. You can maximize your productivity with minimal effort. Learn how to use these tips and tricks!

Chapter 6.   BASIC DEFINITION AND TERMINOLOGY

Basic definition and terminology are a central topic of this book. The lesson's purpose is to learn how to use Microsoft Excel functions to perform standard data analysis and business calculations. Logically, for any business professional using Microsoft Excel, basic definition and terminology skills will be key skill that needs to be understood to work efficiently and effectively in their role. It may not seem like it now but mastering this concept can make all the difference in your career.

Here are the central topics this book will cover:

- Using the Ribbon
- Creating a spreadsheet from scratch
- Formatting cells and text in Excel
- Formatting the worksheet

If you use Microsoft Office 365, you have a copy of Office 2016 with the latest version of Excel installed. One significant difference in this version is that it supports a Ribbon interface instead of the traditional menu system found in previous versions. This Ribbon interface features icons for common commands and other tools to work quickly and efficiently. This part will go over how to use the Ribbon to create a spreadsheet from scratch, format cells and text in Excel, and other basic definitions and terminology.

USING THE RIBBON

The basic idea behind the Ribbon interface is that all the tools, menus, and buttons are organized in a vertical column directly on top of the spreadsheet. This column has a row of self-explanatory icons in most cases, and they can be run through a command by clicking on them, such as the Insert Ribbon icon. Icons for the most common controls, such as Cut, Copy, Paste, and Print. It also shows a particular tool relevant to the task you're doing. For example, if you're formatting text in Excel on a spreadsheet, it will show a drop-down menu that contains options for formatting the text in that column.

The Ribbon is organized into groups of related tasks and tools. The groups are:

Home: Contains the options for formatting cells and text, inserting new columns and rows, using AutoFormat options, and inserting comments.

Insert: Contains the options for inserting objects into the spreadsheet-like tables, charts, or SmartArt. Object insertion is covered later in this tutorial.

Page Layout: Contains only two groups of commands that deal with how the entire spreadsheet prints on paper. It doesn't deal with how individual cells print out on a printer.

Formulas: Contains the groups to add new cells to the spreadsheet, set up functions and formulas, and create data tables. These are covered later in this tutorial.

Data: Contains the groups for dealing with types of data in the spreadsheet, such as sorting, filtering, or using PivotTables. These are covered later in this tutorial.

Analyze: Contains two groups that deal with how Excel deals with data analysis calculations and charts. You can find out more about charts later in this tutorial.

Review: Contains the groups for working with comments and reviews. There are two other groups to print out the worksheet to a printer or save and share data.

View: Contains the groups for viewing a spreadsheet and customizing the screen elements.

Developer: Contains the groups using Visual Basic to customize Excel, create your tools, or use macros.

Tools: Contains the groups for exporting data to PDF, export data to picture, data to XML, and other tools.

The Ribbon also has tabs along its top, which will change depending on what task you're doing. For example, when you're using a cell to enter text, the Home tab will have options for formatting the text. But if you have a chart selected on the screen, it will display tabs with commands specifically relevant to that chart. The Ribbon can also be customized to show only the relevant commands or tools you want to use most often. You can customize the Ribbon by choosing the Home tab and then clicking on any of its icons. This will set up a drop-down menu that contains other options for commands and tools available on that tab. Once you've got the extend of using the Ribbon and its layout, it's relatively intuitive and easy to use. It would be best to remember that there is more than one way to perform specific tasks in Excel. These groups are essential to learning about since they contain unique commands and tools that you need to master to be proficient in Excel. The goal of this part of the tutorial is to go over and understand the various groups on the Ribbon and how it works.

CREATING A SPREADSHEET FROM SCRATCH

This is a tremendous place to start if you're learning how to use the Ribbon in Excel. Open the program and create a fresh spreadsheet by selecting 'New → Blank Workbook' from the File menu. If you use Office 365, this will most likely be called Blank Workbook.

Once created, you'll see the first few rows of cells at the top of the screen. The first row will be the 'Title' row and is usually used to give instructions or outline the purpose of your spreadsheet. Below this is a group called 'Rows' that has basic information about what information is in each column. The actual data itself follow this.

To add data to a row, you first need to select it. You can do this by clicking on the empty cell in that row or highlighting the entire row of cells if they're contiguous (meaning there are no empty cells in between). If a cell is highlighted in red, Excel has automatically entered data into that cell for you. This is called a 'formula,' and it's covered later in this tutorial.

To add data to a cell, you'll need to select the cell first. Click on any cell in the row, or right-click and then choose 'Select' or anywhere else on your sheet that contains a cell. Then you can start typing in the data in the cells. If there are no empty cells between two of these cells, Excel automatically adjusts them to fit your data. You can also have your keyboard shortcuts to quickly jump between rows and columns without having to scroll up and down or use any menus or toolbars. The entire purpose of creating a spreadsheet is to store data to be viewed, manipulated, and analyzed.

Once you have your data sorted correctly, analyzing the data becomes easy. Excel has tools that allow you to quickly see how your data is arranged, how it compares across groups and groups within a category, or how changes in the values of a column affect other columns or the total.

FORMATTING CELLS AND TEXT

The options available will depend upon what type of cell it is, for example, a number or text entry. You can also set custom sizes and styles here in most cases. The easiest way to format cells and text is by using the button found in the Home tab. This is the 'Cells Dropdown.' It contains formatting options relevant to the entire sheet, so they can be used to format any cells in a spreadsheet.

Just click on any cell, or highlight some of them, and this menu should pop up.

Below stands a list of most of the standard formatting options:

- Bold
- Strikeout
- Italicize
- Underline

Apply to Selection and Apply to Entire Selection.

To adjust the font type in cells, you'll need to click on the 'Font' dropdown and then choose the one you want.

Notice that this dropdown menu is different from the other one. This is because it isn't specific to a single cell or a group of cells; instead, it contains formatting options relevant to all fonts and text in your spreadsheet. You should also see how this affects the text once you apply it.

The 'Style' dropdown only contains two options: Normal and Classic. To change the size or style of text, you can also use this option. The different styles will be explained later in this tutorial.

There are numerous other options for styling cells, but most of them aren't used often, so we'll go over them later in the tutorial.

FORMATTING THE WORKSHEET

The "**Number**" dropdown only contains one option: 'Normal.' This is used for formatting cells and numbers on the spreadsheet. It will change the color of the number, add a decimal point, and add lines to make it easier to read large numbers. The other options are used for formatting text (for example, bold or italicized).

The "**Currency**" dropdown contains the same options as the 'Number' dropdown, except it adds an extra option for using a specific currency symbol in numbers. This is usually used for accounting or business applications.

The "**Percentage**" dropdown works similarly to the other formatting options, except that it will format cells as percentages instead of currency or numbers. This is useful since it displays values in comparison to 100% instead of a certain number or currency amount.

The "**Font**" option can be used to change the size, type, or style of any text on the spreadsheet.

The **"Alignment"** dropdown contains all the other options for formatting and aligning text. Left, Center, Right, Top and Bottom.

When used on their own, they will only align single cells that you select. If you choose multiple cells, they will all be aligned in the same direction (for example, all right-aligned or center-aligned).

Using the **'Drawing Tools'** group

The Drawing Tools group contains tools used to draw, resize, or delete data on a sheet. The menu bar above of a sheet is only used to display the commands and tools you can use in each group. The drawing tools are no exception; the menu that pops up when you click on the Drawing Tools button will contain all the options.

A few other valuable things you can do with drawing tools draw a specific shape over an existing shape or select an area on a sheet and then copy it to another location on the page (for example, if you want to create a table of contents at the beginning of your spreadsheets).

The **"Borders and Shading"** option adds a border around a cell that you select. This can be useful for highlighting the value of a cell or simply giving cells more emphasis on your spreadsheet. The options are the same as the 'Borders' option in the Format Cells dropdown menu; you can choose to have a 'Line', 'Dashed Line', 'Dash-Dot Line', or nothing around your cells.

The last part is used for changing the color and style of borders on individual cells. To reform the color of a cell, you first need to select the cell and then click on the 'Fill Color' option. This will show a panel where you can choose different shades of color. The 'No Fill' option is used to delete the color from a cell and make it white (or whatever color your text is).

The **"Conditional Formatting"** option adds certain effects to cells based on their values. It is not used often, but it can be useful for highlighting certain values with color or changing the cells style, size or borders.

This menu has three main options:

- New Rule

- Edit Rule
- Delete Rule.'

The **"New Rule"** option will allow you to add new rules, which allows you to format multiple cells at once with the same setting (for example, all text in the cell should be bold). You can select from the different options under this group, including setting how many spaces to leave after a period or comma and the font used for it.

The **"Edit Rule"** option is used for adding new conditional formatting rules. This will give you access to even more settings and options.

The **"Delete Rule"** option is like 'Edit Rule,' but it will remove all the conditional formatting rules from your current sheet, which can be helpful if you don't want specific cells to have certain effects.

There are also two other options for setting or deleting a rule in this menu. The **"Remove All Rules"** option will delete all the rules and conditionals you currently set on your sheet. The other option, **"Manage Rules"** will launch a new window where you can set even more rules for a specific number of cells. It's not used often, but it is helpful for setting specific effects for large sets of data.

The **'Merge and Center'** option is used for merging cells to the left and right of a selected cell. This command can be helpful when you have data that spans several columns or rows and want to make it fit in a particular area.

The **'Unmerge'** option will reverse 'Merge and Center', which will separate merged cells back into individual ones. Merged cells only remain the same after they are merged. If you change the content of a previously merged cell, then it will no longer be merged when you unmerge it.

The **'Wrap Text'** option is used for wrapping the text in a cell to the next line. This is useful if a cell contains something too long to fit in it (for example, a company name that is longer than the cell itself).

The **'Fill'** option is used for filling in empty cells to the left, right, above or below a selected cell. This is useful if you have data that partially fills a cell and want the remaining content to appear in empty cells beside it.

The **'Interior'** option is used to change the background or interior of a selected cell. It will also allow you to change things like the shading and style.

The **'Toggle Cell Names'** option is used to toggle the display of each cell's name on or off. The names are what you would typically see in a spreadsheet, which can make it easier to use and identify cells (for example, if you don't know where a column is being displayed or what data it has). To toggle the names on or off simply click on this button (it will toggle the feature on and off). To display the cell's name again, click on this button once more (the characters will be shown in a thin black box next to each cell).

The **'Toggle Formula Auditing'** option is used for adding an auditing style to your spreadsheet. This adds a box around the cells you have manually entered your data in (for example, if you have filled in all the data or used a formula to update your data). It can be helpful if you want to highlight certain things or simply add a visual effect.

The **'Toggle Formula Bar'** option will display a blue bar at the bottom of your spreadsheet. This is like the Auditing style; in that it shows which cells have been manually entered into and which cells have been filled with a formula. It can be helpful for people who use formulas often as it gives them an easier way to find where their data is coming from (instead of searching every cell individually).

The **'Insert'** option is used for inserting comments, images and shapes into your spreadsheets. This option will bring up a new panel to insert these objects. You can always add comments at the end of your worksheets, but they are often not seen by other people or they may be too long to be relevant. The images and shapes are useful for adding tiny graphics or icons in your workbook to make it more aesthetically pleasing.

There are two dissimilar styles that you can use for inserting an image or shape in a cell: 'Insert Shapes' and 'Insert Pictures'. The 'Insert Shapes' option will allow you to insert shapes that can be used for things like borders and glares. These can look good, depending on what you are trying to do with it. The 'Insert Pictures' option will insert images into a cell. This allows you to use images that can be quite complex and make your spreadsheet look interesting (for example, an image of a map of the world).

The **'Create a Comment'** option is used for adding a comment to your spreadsheet. Comments are usually used to describe the content of a cell and what each number or formula means. They can also ask someone else a question about the data. This is useful when you want people to see what your data means without looking at all of it first.

The right-most button on this panel, 'Change Comment,' is used for editing an existing comment in your spreadsheet.

The **'Add Attachment'** option adds external files to your spreadsheet. This is useful if you want to comprise an image or a large amount of text somewhere else. To set this, you will need to add the file that you are uploading into the same folder as your spreadsheet, then go to the 'Insert' option, and from where it has been attached, you can use it.

The **'Add a Chart'** option is meant for adding charts to your spreadsheet. Charts can be used to display any data in the world (other than numbers). They are usually used to show icons, pictures, maps, or data that needs a visual representation.

The options discussed so far are primarily used for formatting and adding extra features to spreadsheets. This will help you make your workbook the way you want it. The rest of the buttons on this panel are mainly used for analyzing data and finding specific information. These options are not very important to make your workbook look good, but they can be helpful if you want to analyze it.

Chapter 7.   DATA PRESENTING TECHNIQUES

Presentation plays an integral part in any field - including statistics and data analysis. In general, data visualization is a framework for analyzing data, presenting the results, and learning more about the underlying factors.

There are many dissimilar ways to view the data in your spreadsheet. You can let the data tell for itself, or you can choose to analyze it and extract knowledge from it. This is a material of personal preference, and you should use whatever displays your results in the best way.

DATA VISUALIZATION

The idea of data visualization is to present large quantities of numerical information in meaningful ways to the human eye. The use of data visualization techniques can help you communicate your findings statistically, reduce stress caused by large amounts of information, and improve productivity.

The Benefits: Data Visualization Techniques

Improve accuracy: Make sure your data is reliable by presenting it visually. It is easier to see where errors are in your work - find them earlier and save time.

Save time: Reduce the amount of time spent analyzing data by presenting it visually. - Reduce stress: Data visualization techniques can help alleviate stress caused by large amounts of information and improve productivity.

Communicate results: Presenting a paper visually, rather than just with text, is more exciting and engaging for readers.

Enhance learning: Visualization tools help learn about data.

Stay organized: If a visualization helps keep you organized, then it can help you stay organized.

Reduce stress caused by large amounts of information: You will feel less stressed if you can make sense of the huge volume of information and identify patterns in your data. - Make complex concepts easier to understand: Sometimes, we struggle to understand significant ideas because they are difficult to explain verbally, even with simple diagrams. Visualization can help make complex ideas more understandable.

DATA VALIDATION

Many types of errors can occur during data entry. These include: - Data entry errors: Dropping a digit, transposing two numbers, etc. While entering the data, it's easy to make mistakes that may not be obvious to you until much later.

Quantitative errors: The most common quantitative mistake is when someone puts the wrong number in a cell. Simple multiplication or division of cells can easily result in an incorrect value.

Value errors: A value error occurs when someone inputs a data type that Excel doesn't recognize. This can happen when someone misuses a function, or it could be an entirely new function.

Content errors: These are errors that occur with the content of the data itself. It could be characters in a string exceeding the capacity of the cell (less than 255 characters) or an invalid name, text, or logical value.

Type Mismatch: This is an error that occurs when someone attempts to enter the wrong type of data in a specific cell. For example, you can't put a number into a cell designated for text.

Logical errors occur when someone inputs a value for one thing, but Excel interprets it to mean something else.

Data type errors: This is like the type mismatch error, except Excel recognizes the data as being in the wrong format.

Validation rules

Validation rules are set up to make sure the accuracy of your data. In the case of Excel, you can use validation rules to set up certain functions and formulas so that they will only be carried out if the input is correct. You can have validation rules for ranges, columns, and individual cells. If a validation rule exists for a cell, it won't accept an entry unless it complies with that rule.

Data integrity: Data integrity is when your data doesn't have any errors or problems. You should have validation rules for data integrity to ensure sloppy or careless data entry does not ruin your work.

Accuracy: In Excel, a validation rule is called an error rule. It ensures that your cell entries are accurate and not just any old random string.

Find and fix errors: You attempt to find and fix errors that occur when you enter the data into your spreadsheet. Most of them will appear as minor errors that can be corrected later by editing the worksheet or changing the cell with the error. However, you will also want to prevent the mistakes from occurring in the first place.

Prevent errors: Validation rules are a good tool in your spreadsheet to prevent data entry errors. However, you also should spend lots of time ensuring that all the data entered your spreadsheet is accurate and proper. Some familiar sources of errors include typos, logical fallacies, and invalid function calls.

Here are some tips to teach you effectively present your data:

Color coding: Most people appreciate color coding, as it makes it easy to see patterns in the data. Typically, you use color to represent sales, expenses, and gross profit.

Shapes: There are many shapes in the Excel library that you can use to organize your data visually. For example, if you want to display a pie chart for each quarter of your data, you can map out the pie charts in a column and then outline them with a single shape.

Gridlines: You can hide gridlines or show them as dotted lines (this makes it easier to see the boundaries between columns). The grid lines can be used to create a 2D graph or used in a 3D graph.

BAR(graph): This is a bar graph because it has one dominant value and multiple values that fall on top of the principal value. You can make your bar graphs easier to read by centering the bars within their columns and showing the above or below the bars.

Atlas: An atlas represents data from multiple source documents as one big picture. An atlas allows you to see the relationships between various data sources.

Timelines: A timeline allows you to organize your data based on dates. This makes it smoother for viewers to see patterns in the data.

Clustering: Clustered charts group similar data items together in a single bar or column, making it easier to see patterns and trends within that grouping.

3D: 3D is a way to present data in a manner that is easy to read and understand.

Data Visualization can help the visually impaired navigate through data in a meaningful way. Data visualization projects aim to give people who cannot access visual information and use assistive technology a chance to understand the data presented.

DATA PRESENTING TECHNIQUES:

Data Analysis- Spreadsheets are great, but what if we're trying to present our data in a more digestible and aesthetically appealing way? If that sounds like something you're in, you might want to brush up on your Excel skills. So, are you ready to be an Excel master?

Four Techniques for Presenting Data

1. Visual Profit Chart

This is pretty much like a visual histogram, only instead of giving percentages, the scale is a logarithmic one. The idea is to show the "distribution" of your data. So instead of just showing the percent difference between two points, you can visualize everything in a percentage-less way by using this technique.

2. Insightful Pivot Tables

Excel allows you to create pivot tables that show insights into your work. It's a good idea to use simple colors (red, yellow, and green) to denote positive/negative values. You can also use it to create a visual table of data sorted by specific criteria. Not only does this method make the data easier to process, but it also gives a more visual presentation.

3. Showing Change with Formulas

This is where using the IF function helps. In a spreadsheet, it is possible to create a formula to change the color of cells depending upon what factors you choose. For example, you can change color depending on whether the sales are increasing or decreasing.

4. Categorizing with Chart Groups

Charts are great, but they can get confusing quite quickly. Therefore, it's a good idea to group specific charts so that everything looks more organized and tidier. Not only that, but it's also easy to digest.

If you adore what you do, why not share the love? That's right – since you're efficient at Excel, why not take the time to teach others how to be just like you? Doing so will not only show that they should respect your skills, but it will also give them something valuable in return. Make sure you're performing what you love and teaching others to follow their dreams as well.

Varying Levels of Difficulty

Some Excel tasks are simple, even if you've never touched an Excel spreadsheet in your life. Then, those tasks require a bit more knowledge and practice to complete. Many times, it's best to start on the more accessible side of the spectrum before you move on to more complex topics.

For example, if you want to learn how to create a Pivot Table, it's best not to skip the first step. You don't want to drip the ball in this area and then have no idea what you're supposed to do in the second step. If you can complete step one, it wouldn't be that hard for you to move on with step two.

In the end, you'll be able to do whatever it is that you need to do with Excel.

Asynchronous Processes

If you're just like me, you find yourself working on multiple projects at one time, with one thing constantly distracting you from working on something else. If you place one enormous task in front of you at a time, it can be challenging to maintain your focus. The most acceptable way to handle this is to break your larger project into multiple parts. This way, you're able to work on several different things simultaneously, which will help keep you focused on the task at hand. In that way, you won't be distracted by something else while completing a project.

The only headache with this method is that it might take longer to complete a project because you're splitting your focus, but it's better this way than the alternative. You can always work on one task at a time after all your "pieces" have been completed.

One of the huge gest reasons people don't work as effectively as they can is because they try to complete everything all at once. Also, they continuously restructure their projects as they go. By splitting up your work into different parts, you force yourself to complete each one of these separate tasks. This helps you stay on task and prevent distractions from other projects that may be going on simultaneously.

Here are a few different techniques that can help improve your efficiency in Excel:

1.   Work with Multiple Projects at Once

When you're on a large project, it's possible that several parts of it can be completed simultaneously. There might be some tasks that only take a few minutes, so you may as well handle them while you're working on something else. Then other tasks can only be accomplished once those smaller tasks have been finished.

2.   Work with the Same Data in Multiple Spreadsheets

If you're on a large project, the chances are good that there will be several different Excel spreadsheets associated with it. These various spreadsheets might be spread out over several days or even weeks. The best way to handle this work is to always work with the same data in each spreadsheet. This way, if you need to reference it for something else, later, you know where it's located.

A very typical example is if you're creating a sales report. You'll probably want to start by creating a spreadsheet that has all your products listed on it. As you complete each invoice, you'll need to keep this spreadsheet updated with the latest information. Then, you might have another sheet that has all your products listed in it again, but this time it includes their current inventory level. You'll also want to create a report that calculates the difference between these two numbers. Likewise, if you always work with the same data in every spreadsheet throughout your project, everything should fall into place once you're done.

3.   Work with a Time-Based Schedule

This is one of the leading ways to ensure you're staying on task. If you're working on different parts of your project simultaneously, you'll be able to break them up into sections based on their due dates. You can then schedule your work based on how long it will take to complete each part. This will help you avoid procrastinating and keep yourself on track. Some people can also use their schedule as a reward for completing certain portions of their work.

Chapter 8.   BASIC FUNCTIONALITIES

Most features and functions are the most widely used spreadsheet application for personal and business purposes. The application has retained its popularity because of its simplicity, reliability, and flexibility. Across the world, people use Excel to organize data to make informed decisions for their businesses. It is now the most used spreadsheet application. In this section, we've compiled a list of most features and functions available in excel for you to know. Excel also equips you with the ability to create charts. This enables you to change the way your data is represented so that you can easily visualize it. For this feature, Excel supports both different 2D and 3D charts, allowing you to create visual representations of your data in 2D and 3D formats. Whether you want to create a pie chart, histogram, or even gauge bars, this program allows you to do so in just a few minutes.

ADDING NEW ROWS AND COLUMNS

In Excel, you can easily add new rows or columns to your workbook. This way, you can create more detailed analyses of your results. Moreover, this lets you be creative and let more data points be presented simultaneously in a chart. Excel also allows you to hide or move existing rows and columns if necessary for your analysis. Excel also lays out you with the ability to enter and edit content, such as text and numbers. This can be achieved by typing them directly into your worksheets or importing raw text files data.

CREATING CHARTS

To make your work more visually appealing, Excel also provides you with the ability to create different types of charts (line, graph, bar, image). To make your data look more straightforward and more confident, it provides you with various options to alter the appearance of your charts. This lets you adjust the color scheme, column widths, and borders. It also allows you to enhance the aesthetics by adding images to your charts and adding or removing chart elements such as titles or axes.

CALCULATORS

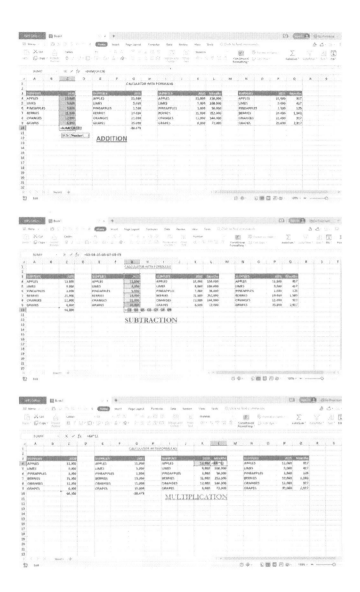

This is the most popular spreadsheet function. It allows for simple addition, subtraction, multiplication, and division. This way, you can efficiently work with numbers without having to open another application.

CONDITIONAL FORMATTING

This feature allows you to create charts and graphs that highlight different aspects of data based on present and past conditions. This is useful for underlining trends and patterns in data or highlighting deviations from essential criteria. Along with conditional formatting, Excel offers a variety of other functions such as percentile charts, pivot tables, charts with multiple series, and more.

TEXT-TO-COLUMNS

This feature allows you to split a text into columns and combine it with other data like numbers or dates. This will enable you to organize numbers and dates into rows instead of columns easily.

COLOR SCHEMES

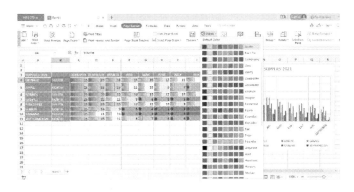

Using this tool, you can automatically color cells based on their values. This way, you can easily visualize a distribution or a trend in your workbook.

AUTOFILTER

This function that highlights rows of data that meet specific criteria. This tool allows you to automatically filter content by replacing specific parts of your data with other data sources. AutoFilter is an excellent feature for quickly filtering data so you can work on what matters most to you at any point in time. This way lets you quickly sort vast amounts of data to display only the most important content. It allows you to filter data by column or row and makes it possible to filter data in multiple directions.

CURSOR

The cursor is the pointer that shows where new text will be entered. This tool can be used to move the cursor to another cell to view another part of your data. This way, it lets you quickly switch between different parts of your workbook without having to use multiple tools.

DRAGGING

You can drag a column's label in a sheet, and the entire column will follow the label. This feature allows you to rearrange parts of your worksheet quickly. It lets you move content between cells, folders, or even other files.

MULTI-THREADING

This feature allows Excel to use the computer's power efficiently by running multiple calculations in parallel. It has a huge impact on the speed you can compute your spreadsheet. This allows you to perform multiple tasks on your computer at the same time. It can add additional features such as spellchecking while typing out text in a cell while keeping the program interface open and accessible.

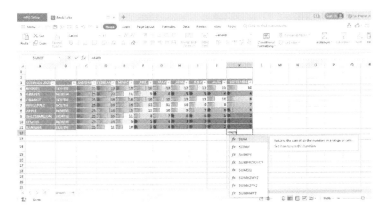

This tool allows you to perform mathematical functions on the values in cells. For example, you can utilize this tool to add, subtract or multiply numbers in a cell.

SORTING

This feature lets you quickly sort content in various ways. It allows you to sort data by its ascending or descending order, for example.

Allows you to install add-ins, which provides additional functionality over the base application. This means you can add tools that can be used to visualize data from multiple sources, retrieve information from the internet, or generate content on the fly.

CELL COMMENTS

This feature allows you to add a comment about a single cell. These comments appear when you hover over the cell and disappear when you move from it. Words are beneficial for data tables, where the comments function as text notes for other users.

DRAWING FREEHAND SHAPES

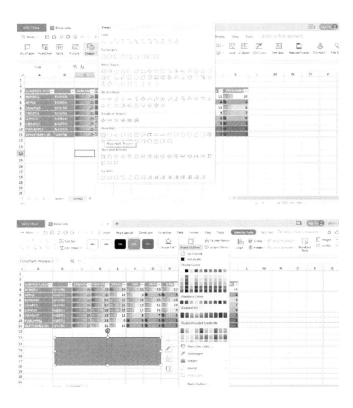

This tool allows you to create freeform patterns in the chart area. These patterns are unique to Excel and can be used to create attractive designs of various types.

Creating dates and dates ranges

This tool allows you to create dates for your charts. Excel's date features are easy to understand and work with. For example, you can create a graph with multiple series and add a date for each series to see trends and patterns in different periods.

Collaborative feature

Excel allows you to share different versions of workbooks with other users, who can then edit the worksheet, save their changes and send them back to you. You can also create password-protected files that prevent other users from making changes to the file.

CUSTOMIZING RIBBONS

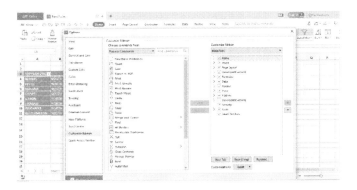

The ribbon is the toolbar that appears at the top of a workbook. Users can customize the ribbons by adding and removing tabs and rearranging tabs. It can contain a variety of commands for you to use in your workbook, from formatting cell contents to inserting graphs.

IMPORTING AND EXPORTING DATA

This feature allows you to import data from other sources (such as XML files) and export information into other formats (such as HTML) that are more effective for publishing purposes. You can import other Excel spreadsheets into the one you are working on so that you can quickly perform calculations on this enormous collection of data. You can also export information to another workbook so that you can work on other projects without losing your current project.

This feature allows you to copy a cell that contains text and convert it into a cell that uses numbers, dates, or formulas. This is convenient if you want to automate the process of replacing text with various types of data.

Excel is a powerful tool that can be used to analyze vast amounts of data. By creating a suitable workbook, you can analyze data from different sources and visualize it to make it accessible and easy to understand. With a few clicks, you can generate charts and graphs which look appealing and show clear trends in your data. Using this tool, you can easily organize and manipulate your data to present it in a more understandable form. To help you visualize your data, knowing how to work with Excel is a good start. However, the right way of working with Excel depends on everyone. Therefore, being aware of its advantages and disadvantages can be helpful when making the different choices that come with this software.

In general, if you realize that Excel can give you more options for displaying your work or let you get around complicated issues.

Chapter 9. FORMATTING

If you're fed up with the similar, boring Excel grid and labels, it's time to get creative. Various formatting tools can be used to make your spreadsheet into a work of art — and we're here to show you how.

CHARACTERS, COLORS, SIZE

Formatting excel is not easy on Excel. But there is a way you can make it easier by using some predefined patterns and styles. This way, you only need to apply the techniques you like to your spreadsheet. Characters and designs can be copied and pasted into other cells without using the styles each time. Each type is a set of preset formatting settings. The point of styles is to save you time by applying the same formatting to an entire spreadsheet. Storing these styles in the same document with the text formatting is beneficial for two reasons. First, working with many different documents with similar formatting requirements will know precisely where each style lives. And second, if you forget what a style is called, at least it will be easy to remember which one is called "Styles." Styles are applied on top of the existing text formatting so that more than one format can be used to a cell or block of cells at any given time. Styles are beneficial for applying consistent design to any document, but they accommodate formatting an Excel spreadsheet. Out of the box, Excel comes with many predefined styles that can be applied to any block of text to format it appropriately quickly. This is the easiest way to apply consistent formatting throughout an entire workbook. Fonts and size are the most used styles to format a spreadsheet quickly. With styles, you can also specify how each style is applied to text in the cell. Let's say you want the first word in each cell to be bolded, but the remaining words should be italicized. Usually, you would have to apply both styles individually for each word. But with styles, all you need to do is select one of the predefined options that combines these two settings.

To do this, select the data you want formatted. It can be one row of data or multiple rows - it doesn't matter because any changes that are made will apply to all of them simultaneously. From there, click on 'format' then on 'cells.' Then, on the 'home' tab, you'll see several different sections. To change your font size, you can either click on the drop-down arrow next to the font listed and select a new font size from the list or click directly onto the font size box and enter a new size into that box.

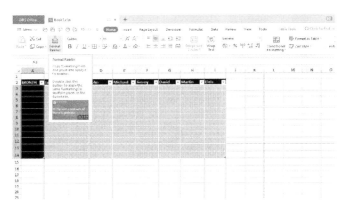

To change the color of your font, if you click on the drop-down arrow next to the font listed and select a different color from this list, or you can click directly onto the font color box and enter a new color into that box.

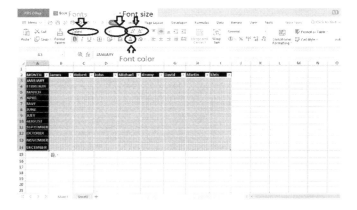

No matter what kind of formatting you're looking for, there's an option that will fit the bill. Be creative with your formatting styles, and they can help you create unique spreadsheets that are easy on the eye.

ALIGNMENT, MERGE, WRAP

You can take your cells in Excel and push them around to get the look you aim for. Alignment Merging and wrapping are similar, but there are a few differences. The first action you should know is that alignment changes the spacing between columns or cells within a column, making your spreadsheet more readable. It allows you to align left, right, or center. It also allows you to align cells vertically, which we will go over in the next section. The default option for alignment is left, but it can be changed to right or center. If you want to align over one cell at a time, you can merge the cells and wrap text and other objects. These two actions are grouped as the wrapped group of the alignment group; they don't get confused with each other. By default, all three options (Alignment, Merge, and Wrap) are turned off. Once they're enabled, you can align, wrap or merge any cell using the buttons on the bottom row of cells in the row and column headers.

You use the alignment command by clicking on a cell and then expanding the alignment button at the bottom of your spreadsheet. There are five options: left, right, center, justify, and vertical. The justify option creates two columns instead of one. This makes the cells the same height, but they sit on top of each other. If you ought to center your text vertically in your cell, click on the vertical alignment icon and select 'center.' It's convenient for when you want your columns to align vertically. This is not feasible in all cases; if you need that, then don't hesitate to use the wrap option instead.

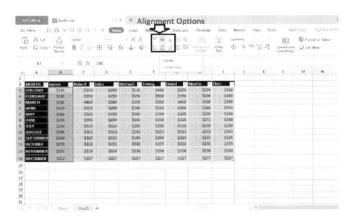

It's imperative to have wrapped text or objects that are not on top of each other. Wrap smoothing tries to automatically adjust column widths when there are too many rows between them, which can help prevent gaps along the side. The default spacing is 10 characters; however, you can change that with the wrap width. When wrapped text or objects are too close to each other, they can look ugly. If you need to make the corner of a picture, go all the way around it properly, use wrapping. This can also help if your text spans multiple columns. If you have a lot of wrap lines in your spreadsheet, they will pile up at the bottom of your screen and take up valuable real estate. You can change this by adjusting the wrap margin. The default is 0 characters, but you can also choose a number, which will keep a certain number of wrap lines from being shown. You can hide those extra lines from view using the hide wrap option. The same thing applies to merged cells.

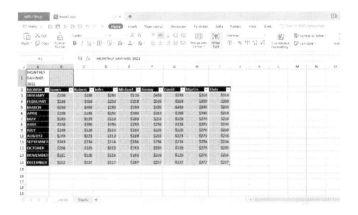

While merged cells are slightly different from wrapped cells, they do share some things in common. Merged cells also sit on top of each other, and they also have a small gap between them that you can't get rid of if it bothers you. Sometimes it is necessary to merge cells. Wrap lets you change the orientation of text within its cell, either horizontally or vertically. The rotate tool allows you to rotate numbers or text in their cells. This gap is only visible when you are looking at the spreadsheet in print mode. You can't change the margin on merged cells, but you can make it smaller with the move cells to justify the option.

The wrapping and aligning options are similar, but they aren't the same, so let's go over them one at a time. Justify is self-explanatory; it just makes sure that your cells are all the same height.

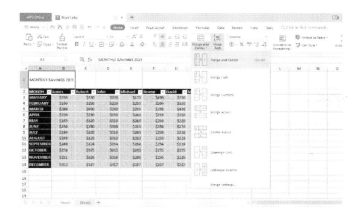

There are a lot of ways to make your spreadsheets more readable. We have already discussed the alignment, merge, and wrap features that are built into Excel. There are also different methods to improve your spreadsheet stand out from the crowd. Alignment, merge, and wrap are all handy tools to help you get the most out of your spreadsheet. These simple options are more than just ways to make it look more professional, and they are ways to improve your spreadsheet.

ALL CELL DATA TYPES AND COMMON ISSUES

The world of spreadsheets is changing year after year, and so is the way you should format your cells. Many common issues arise when including dates in your Excel spreadsheet, such as displaying numbers as dates. There are many little updates and rules that come into play that can surprisingly change how you should format cells in Excel every few months. In this part we will look at the most common issues you may encounter, and how to best work around them. There is no better time than right now to get up to date with the new formatting rules in Excel.

First, you'll need to know that cell formatting in Excel is done in two ways: By using Formatting Cells and by using formatting your data. Formatting your data is the technique we generally recommend. It's more flexible and you can have a lot more control on how Excel will display your data. However, Formatting Cells is still necessary in certain cases so you know what Excel will do with your data when it tries to format it.

Excel has a different format for each data type:

Dates: Short: dd/mm/yy (example: 01/04/2016) Medium: d mmmm, yyyy (example: Jan 4, 2016) Long: dddd, mmmmm yy (example: Wednesday, January 04, 2016)

Time: hh: mm :ss (example: 1 :49 :23 PM)

Numeric: 0,,-,,+,-,.# (example: 4,478.4)

Currency: $#,##0.00 (example: $1,000.5)

Percentage: 0%,#0% (example: 0%,20%)

Fraction: 1/2 = 0.5, 1/4 = 0.25

Formatting your data is easy. To include a date in your spreadsheet you need to use either the short / medium / long format. The exact format used depends on how you entered it (if entered as text, like hh:mm by date or mm/dd/yy then the short format is used; if entered as numbers then the medium or long format will be used).

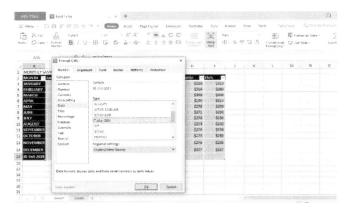

When Excel tries to format a cell, it looks at the contents of the cell and makes a best guess as to what format would make the contents easier to read. So perhaps the most important thing to know is that Excel will try to display data in the way it expects it.

CONDITIONAL FORMATTING AND TABLE FORMAT

Most spreadsheet applications have conditional formatting options. You can filter what to show or hide when the conditions are met for your data. Some of these are cool visual ways to simplify your work without even needing to know any formulas. But what if you want an infographic? This is where table formatting comes in handy because it allows you to enter multiple data types into a single column. When entering values, each cell has its format depending on the type of data in the column.

This part will provide information on how to use these two functions in tandem to create elegant and informative spreadsheets that are visually appealing and easy to read, no matter the size of the screen, be it large or small.

1. Conditional formatting on single columns

There are 4 conditional formatting functions for single columns called:

Table format function: Used to create unique customized table formats for your data. Highlighting cells matching the criteria is the main purpose of this function.

List format functions: Used to create custom table formats using the same function as the table format one.

List boxes: Used for creating data-heavy displays where list boxes are used for displaying values. List boxes are 2-dimensional. When you use them, you cannot change or reorder columns in your data list or click on individual cells within the list box to edit them directly. If you do not specify any formatting rules, Excel will apply the default formatting rules of your selected data set.

2. Conditional formatting on multiple columns

There are 3 conditional formatting functions for multiple columns that allow you to group related cells together. Only 1 of the functions has the option to highlight rows according to specified conditions.

---

3. Conditional formatting with table format

Conditional formatting with table format is used for creating unique customized table formats for your data. Highlighting cells matching the criteria is the main purpose of this function.

- Click the table format icon in the toolbar or press Ctrl+Alt+L
- Click on one of the following options:

Table Column: to enter values in multiple rows at once.

Table Drop Down list: to enter values in multiple rows at once using a dropdown menu.

Table Widget Boxes: quickly creating conditional formatting rules with different formatting colors based on each data type and cell value combination.

- In the conditional formatting dialog box, specify what you want to be highlighted and additional options such as format color, font size, style, and background color.
- Excel will automatically highlight the cells that meet all the conditions specified. If you want to highlight additional cells that meet some or all your conditions, then select 3-conditions in the dialog box and click on the Plus icon.
- Click OK and see how your data looks like now!

4. Conditional formatting with the list format

Conditional formatting with list format is used for creating custom table formats using the same function as with table format one. Use it to make a stellar data display in your PowerPoint presentations, slide shows, or a PPTX file.

- Click the list style icon in the toolbar or press Ctrl+Alt+L
- Use this dialog box to enter information in your data lists by specifying how you want your data lists to appear. If you use the

same format throughout the list, you will need to select only one item for each format type.

- Once you have entered all your formatting rules, check on the Show box near the top of the dialog box so that Excel will highlight each cell that meets all these formatting conditions.
- Click OK and see how your data looks like now!
- In the conditional formatting dialog box, specify what you want to be highlighted and additional options such as format color, font size, style, and background color.

5. **Conditional formatting with list boxes**

Conditional formatting with list boxes is used to create data-heavy displays where the list boxes are used to display values within each section of the list box. Here's an example:

- Click the Listbox icon in the toolbar or press Ctrl+Alt+L
- Click on one of the following options. The first option has all the conditional formatting rules already set, so you can just click on it, and your data will appear as follows:
- In the conditional formatting dialog box, specify what you want to be highlighted and additional options such as format color, font size, style, and background color.

Conditional formatting is an easy way to give your Excel data sets life by making them more visually appealing. It allows you to highlight specific cells to present data in a clear, understandable way. By using these three functions together, you can create visual art while also skimming the information.

ADD AND REMOVE COLUMNS/CELLS

We all start with a spreadsheet, but sometimes we need to add columns or cells for new data. Here's a quick step to get you started!

How do I add a column?

In Excel 2020, click the "Insert" tab from the Ribbon and select "insert column." You can also right-click where you want the new column to go and click "insert." In either case, choose "right" for vertical spacing or left" for horizontal spacing.

How do I delete a column?

Click the "Insert" or "Manage" tab from the Ribbon, locate the column you want to remove and choose "delete column." You can also right-click where you would like to remove the column and click "remove," or right-click in an empty cell and select "delete."

How do I add a cell?

Locate the row you want to add to, click on the bottom right corner of an unoccupied cell in the row and drag down.

How do I delete a cell?

Right-click on an empty cell where you want to remove a cell and choose "delete." You can also use the "Remove" tab from the Ribbon.

Creating a new worksheet in Excel can be handy, especially when you keep track of multiple projects and keep everything separate. Also, you can add and delete rows and columns as per your needs. In a world where people are constantly hungry for information, the demand for Excel knowledge has never been greater. But being a master of Excel is not as easy as it seems and takes many skills that may come normally to you.

Chapter 10.   MERGING CELLS IN EXCEL USING THE MERGE COMMAND

Merging cells in excel using the merge command is a helpful way to keep your data tidy and organized. But if you don't know how the merge command works, you might find yourself working through endless strings of formulas. This chapter will show you how the merge command works and how to use it to keep your data neat.

A cell can be separated into up to three areas. These areas are called "regions." Each region has a different name and purpose. The title of each region is written on the cell. Both regions are important to keeping your data organized. You want to separate these regions like this so that you don't accidentally update one of the cells by accident. For example, if you accidentally change the data in a cell that is part of the title, it will update all the cells below it when you click on the title cell.

The section heading is used to describe each region. The first letter of the heading is used as a prefix.

Bear in mind that if you delete a section heading, the merge command will update your data, and it won't create an extra column. This is because the commands are designed for merging cells, not creating separate columns. Also, bear in mind that if you set up your worksheet without separating your regions properly and then decide to tidy it up, you can fix it by using the "clean worksheet" option on the "edit" menu.

HOW THE MERGE COMMAND WORKS

When running a merge command, the program uses shortcuts to identify what cells are part of which regions. This is how the merge command creates two new columns. Here's the things that occur when you run a merge command:

1. The first thing that happens is that any merged cells are automatically moved to the new column. This way, all merged cells will show up in the same cell after merging.

2. Next, the program counts how many times each region appears. If a range has multiple instances of the same region, it is added to that cell once and then removed.

3. Now, the program looks for any blank cells in your data. These cells are all added to the column of the first instance of a region.

4. If any cells don't have a heading, they will be added directly to this column as well. You can use the "clean worksheet" option to tidy up this data.

5. The last thing that happens is that the cells in your previous columns are shifted down to make room for the new columns. This is done one row at a time, starting with the row with the highest number of heading cells.

To merge your data, you can find all cells part of a region and select "merge and center." You can also run a merge command from the edit menu.

MERGING CELLS USING THE CONTENTS MENU

The contents menu is a handy way to run a merge command. If you select the "contents" menu and right-click on a cell part of a region, you'll see options to merge this cell. You can also use the "contents" menu to change the style of your data. By default, all merged cells are in bold and underlined. You can change this by clicking on this option on the contents menu or directly editing your styles.

In today's business world, spreadsheets have become a must-have tool for analyzing information. They are used in nearly every field and industry because they can pull together large amounts of data in one place, sort it, and present it in an easy-to-read format.

Many companies depend on their spreadsheets for accurate, up-to-date information about the financial health of their business. Because of this, it is difficult that you become proficient in creating and working with spreadsheets and maintaining them. This part will give you some tips on doing both things.

- First and foremost, you need to be familiar with the formulas used in the spreadsheet. These formulas are the building blocks of spreadsheet creation, and they will help you teach yourself how to do more advanced things.

- To create spreadsheets that are easy to understand, it is essential that your formulas are easy to read. Ideally, the formula should be directly above the cell it pertains to. This makes it easier for anyone looking at your spreadsheet in the future.

- If you have a lot of data in your spreadsheet, make sure that you use the scroll bar so that no critical information is overlooked. It's essential to note that the scroll bar must be above the formula cell.

- Be sure that when you enter information into a spreadsheet, it is entered in the correct column. Excel may not place it in the right column if you do not use the column menu.

- When entering information, you want to be in the same column, you can use the "equal sign" as a shortcut.

- The "delete" button is used for deleting data in your spreadsheet and pressing entered keys multiple times.

- The "insert" button is used to insert data in your spreadsheet. If your formula takes text from another source, it will be inserted into the correct cell.

- The "format as" option is used to format your spreadsheet. This option can be used with the "format rows" and "format columns" options.

- The "sort" option will sort your data based on your choice of column or row. You can sort by column or row and you can either sort ascending or descending.

- When you are done with a cell, the "delete key" will delete the cell if it is empty. If it contains data, it will not be deleted.

- The "enter" key is used to accept a cell's value and then move to the next cell.

- If you find that your spreadsheet has become too full and you cannot move past a certain cell, click on the "zoom" button and then on "zoom-out." This will allow you to see an entire row or column at once.

- The "arrow keys" are used to move up and down in a column.

- To go back to normal, click on the "reset" button, which will restore your current settings to their original state.

- To go forward from point A to point B, use the arrow keys (up and down) and then press enter, which will put you strictly at your next cell. You will now be able to set through your data in that column or row.

- When working with a spreadsheet, you will need different formats for your data. The "format" button allows you to change how your data is displayed. You can change the font type, font color, and border color. The format button can also be used with other functions such as sort and merge.

These options are designed to make it easy for you to keep your data neat and organized. So, the next time you update your data, you can use a merge command instead of wading through endless strings of formulas.

Chapter 11. INSERTING

One of the new features of Excel 2021 is the option to insert a table into a spreadsheet. Tables are used to organize data in rows and columns.

To insert a table, you need to have your cursor in cell A1 and then click on Insert > Table... from the menu bar. This will open a dialog box where you can specify the size of the table, number of rows, columns and so on.

Some of the most common mistakes in Excel happen when we're trying to insert a table into a spreadsheet is the table being inserted in the wrong cell. To insert a table into the wrong cell, either selects an empty cell or have the editing options turned on. For example, if you are inserting a table that spans two or more rows, it is recommended to insert the table into a column of the same row as in which table you wish to place.

The quick steps below will help you avoid these mistakes and produce a professional-quality table.

1. First, select the area you want to be a table.
2. Then create a table by going to Insert > Table... from the menu bar.
3. A dialog box will appear where you can specify the number of rows and columns.
4. Click OK and you will see your table!

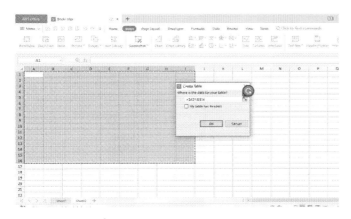

PIVOT TABLE

Pivot table is a fancy Excel term, but it's essentially just a data summarizer. The basic idea behind Pivot tables is to summarize data in the Excel workbook so that you can explore subsets of your data without having to export it to another tool or modify your worksheet.

A pivot table takes raw data and summarizes it in two main ways: by showing summary totals for each field and breaking these totals out into counts of distinct values for each field.

The Pivot Table is an excellent tool for visualizing data, but it often requires patience and skill to extract insights from it! Look for Excel Pivot tables in your workbook, and you will see a collection of them built from the raw data in your workbook. The basic steps are outlined below.

Step 1: Create a Pivot table.

The beginning step is to create a Pivot table to view the data in your workbook. You can make the pivot table from the ribbon menu click "DATA" > "PivotTable."

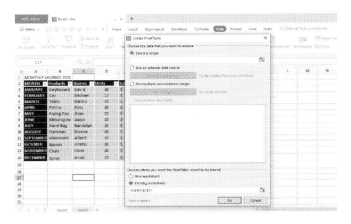

Step 2: Create a Pivot table from a range of cells.

In the next step, you would select the range of data that you want to summarize in your pivot table. This can either be fit by dragging the cursor.

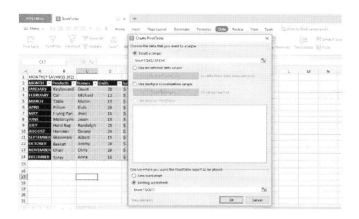

Step 3: Select and define the sort column.

You would then select the column that you want to see information in and click on the arrow in that column. This will highlight the column and shift all data into one line. You must select the sort order for this step because the Pivot table needs to know what type of data is being sorted to process it correctly.

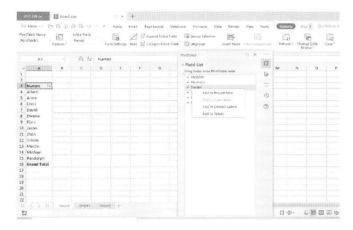

Step 4: Define a summary field that will help you visualize your data quickly.

Repeat the previous step to select the other columns, and you will have a Pivot table that allows you to see your data in aggregate. There are also summaries from different fields that can help you understand what is happening in your data.

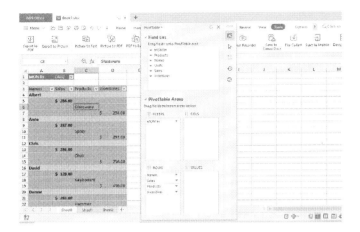

ILLUSTRATION

Inserting illustration in Excel is the process of inserting a picture into your spreadsheet. It can be helpful when you want to represent some data or make text easier to read.

We can insert illustration with the use of insert tab in excel. There are several types of illustrations that you can insert in your spreadsheet: Wordart, text boxes, shapes and pictures. You can also create your own illustration using shapes tool in excel.

Using shapes

When you click on shapes icon from the Insert tab, you will see a list of all available shapes. Choose any shape and drop it into your spreadsheet.

Once you have added a shape, you can select it and use the control handles to adjust the position as you like.

You can also change the size of the shape by clicking on resize handle located at the top right corner of the shape. By changing the size of shapes, you can increase or decrease white spaces around your shapes in your spreadsheet.

If you want to change the color of a shape, you can select it with your mouse and click on the box icon located at the right end of the control handle. The customization pane will show up. Select More fill options at top left corner and choose Fill options button. A new customization pane will appear. Click on color fill button and choose any color to change its default color as you like.

A simple illustration in excel is created.

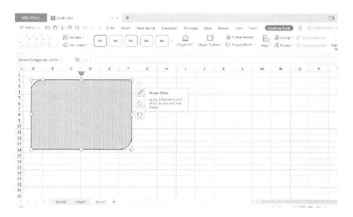

Using textbox

If you want to include some text in your illustration, you can use textbox option. Textbox option is located right next to wordart option in the insert tab. It will let you add text, an image or both into a box and resize the box accordingly. You can place the box anywhere on your spreadsheet.

After adding a textbox, select it with mouse pointer and you will see control handles appear on the box. You can adjust box size, position and color with these handles.

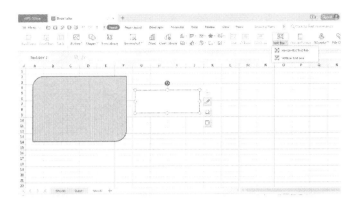

Using wordart

Wordart is a ready-made picture created in word that can be used to illustrate your data. Insert tab has an option called Wordart which will insert a wordart picture in your spreadsheet. Once you click on that option, you will see a list of wordarts to choose from. Select the wordart and it will be inserted in your spreadsheet.

Using Pictures

You can also insert picture from your computer or other devices into excel with the use of insert tab. Just click on Pictures option in the insert tab and choose pictures from your computer or other device that you want to display in your spreadsheet. Once you select pictures, it will be inserted and appear in your spreadsheet.

You can also add picture from a particular website or attachment as shown in the picture below.

To add a picture to a specific cell, you must first select the cell with mouse and then choose insert tab and select pictures option. It will provide you different placeholders. Select the desired placeholder and choose download link of image from your browser.

A simple illustration created using clip art, text box and shapes tool in excel.

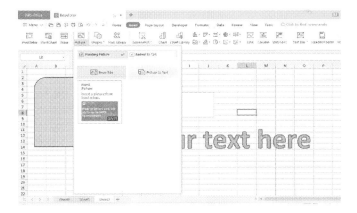

This can be helpful for making charts or even drawings. It's easy for anyone to use and it's great for kids who are learning about shapes and how to change them on their own. Illustration in Excel can be a great tool for designers who want to make spreadsheets that are more visually appealing.

CHARTS

If you are using Excel, it is the best type of graph to use for your report. Charts are graphical representations of statistical information and are used to visualize numerical data. Excel has special types of charts that it provides by default and can enable you to customize the appearance of them in several ways. Charts can be customized with colors, titles, and labels. There are many types of charts that you may want to use in your spreadsheet depending on the data that you have gathered. You can also create a chart yourself or download one from an online source. Here is a list of some more Chart types:

Column Chart: This is used when displaying the relative change in a series of data like sales or cost.

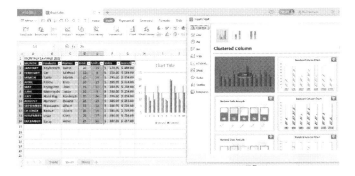

Line chart: This is used to illustrate various changes in your data over time.

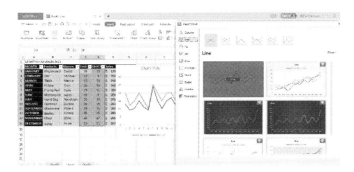

Pie Chart: Is used when displaying parts of whole like percentages or shares.

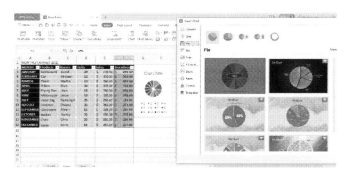

Bar Charts: Are used when you want to represent a series of values for

each category.

Area chart: Is used to show changes in your data over a period, whether it is a rising or falling line.

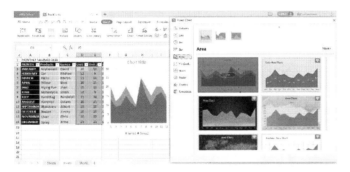

Scatter chart: Is used to show the relationship between two or more variables.

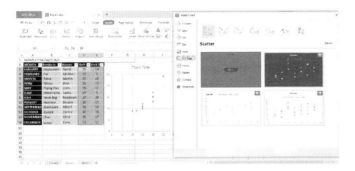

Stock chart: This type of chart is used by new traders to show their potential for a certain stock in the stock markets.

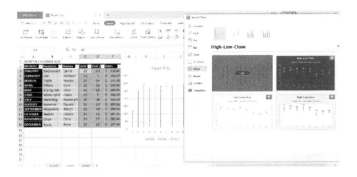

Radar Chart: For presenting changes in your data in a single dimension.

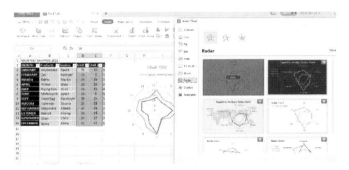

Combo Chart: Is also called time series chart. It is a combination of two different types of charts. It can be used to show changes in data over a period.

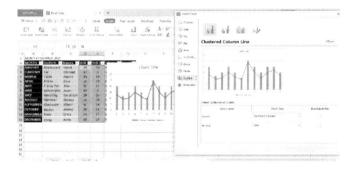

One thing that is cool about them is that they allow you to control how your data looks right down to the last detail. There are so many different types of charts in Excel. One thing they all have in common is that you can customize all the elements of your chart including background, title, data and axes among other things.

Links and comments in excel workbooks are the most common way to supplement a workbook and provide a more interactive experience. This can be anything from a tool for collaboration to providing additional information on an entity or providing comments about the data in your workbook. However, as you build your workbooks, links can also become unwieldy and messy. This is about a method for improving the readability of links in an excel workbook. Specifically, how to improve the formatting of internal links that make up a dashboard or report. This will describe how to format the display of internal links so they are easier to read and follow through a workbook. Before we get into that, let's first cover how to display external links and why internal links are sometimes necessary.

External links in excel workbooks typically function as references to information or values outside of the workbook. This is not always the case, however: you can also have an internal link in a workbook. These are typically used as references between worksheets which serve as navigational aids. For example, you can have one worksheet with all your product names and another worksheet with all your related information. In that case, you can use an internal link between the two sheets to provide a navigational aid to the user. However, if the user clicks on this link, they will just end up back on the same sheet, no matter how far away on your dashboard users are from your desired location. This may seem like a problem, but in fact it can be handy when you have a simple set of worksheets. You can have the first worksheet with all the products and then have another worksheet on top where users navigate to find product descriptions. You can then use an internal link inside the first sheet to get back to that product description sheet.

Links and comments in excel workbooks are the most common way to supplement a workbook and provide a more interactive experience. links can provide more information on a topic or take the reader to another workbook. comments allow the author to leave notes for someone else, like an editor or coworker, without having to interrupt their flow. these are just two ways to help users interact with workbooks.

Comments are limited to 80 characters and may not contain any formatting. they can be added with the insert comment command. comments will be visible to anyone who opens the workbook unless these people have turned off comments in the view tab of the excel options dialog box. comments are viewable in the comments window, while editing the workbook.

How to add comments to an excel workbook

1. Select the cell you want to place the comment in...
2. Use the ribbon's insert tab and click comments
3. Fill-in the comment
4. Apply any formatting or additional information

Links are helpful when a reader needs more detail on a topic or wants to move from page to page. links are dynamic and will automatically change if a worksheet is moved, renamed, or deleted. links cannot be added to cells with merged cells or table elements. links are added in the insert tab under links.

Links can be added on their own, or as part of a hyperlink. a hyperlink is like a link, but it makes a clickable connection to an external file, like another excel workbook or an online web page.

How to add links and hyperlinks in an excel workbook

1. Select the cell you want to place the link/hyperlink in...
2. Use the ribbon's insert tab, and click links or hyperlinks
3. Select your link/hyperlink from the submenu.
4. Fill-in the link parameters.

5. Click OK

Comments are no different than links, except that they appear in the comments window. links may have a hotkey assigned, but comments don't. links and comments can be added using keyboard shortcuts under the insert comment or insert link command. links are limited to 255 characters and may contain formatting. they can be added with the insert hyperlink command. as with comments, links are visible to anyone who opens the workbook, unless these people have turned off links in the view tab of the excel options dialog box.

How to add a link to an excel workbook

1. Click the tab called "Insert" at the top.
2. Click "Hyperlink".
3. Click "Text link".
4. Click one of the following:

Paste text from your spreadsheet in an email or in a document

Paste a hyperlink to any site you want on your spreadsheet

Type it yourself! that's right, type anything you want, even emoji! and then click "OK"

That way users can share their opinions on the topic and other readers can gain more insight into the information they read. Moreover, if you want to advertise your company name or link somewhere in your workbook while retaining anonymity, this function is ideal for you as well.

Chapter 12.   Understanding the Pivot table

Microsoft added other application features to the spreadsheet including pivot tables in version 7.0 and beyond. It turns out, pivot tables are one of the most powerful features at your disposal in Excel, but they operate in a slightly different way than you might have guessed. Here are some tips on how to master this little-understood feature of the most popular spreadsheet program on earth—pivot table. This chapter will level up your Excel knowledge by teaching you how to make a pivot table! Using the commands to accomplish a pivot table, this is the kind of thing you'll be able to tackle after reading this part. This chapter will level up your Excel knowledge by teaching you how to make a pivot table! Using the commands to accomplish a pivot table, this is the kind of thing you'll be able to tackle after reading this part.

What is a Pivot table?

Simply, a Pivot table is a worksheet function that displays the data from multiple rows and columns in a manner that makes it easy to see how your totals break down by different variables. The Word "pivot table" comes from the fact that you can look at your data as though it were mounted on the front of an automobile, with all the numbers stored on different parts of the car. You can then turn the car in any direction and the numbers will appear on the "side" of the table and you can read them.

By default, Excel Pivot tables are set up to display values from two fields, like "sales" and "cost of goods sold," that you select in a separate area of your spreadsheet. If a third field—like "month"—is included in the data you're looking at, Pivot tables will present sales totals for every month. If you have a fourth field, like "market share," it will present all the sales and profits for a third, fourth, fifth or sixth "market segment."

While it's true that Pivot tables show you how your data breaks down in more than one way—and can even include multiple information fields—the big thing about the Pivot table is that it increases your ability to focus on one piece of data without having to take in all the information available. This can be a real time saver when you have a lot of numbers to look at.

Why use pivot tables?

Pivot tables are useful when you want to compare different measures and depending on the measures, you want to present different results, for example. Let say you want to determine which product has done well in sales. You might want to compare sales revenue and the number of products to determine which product is doing better. You might also want to compare the number of sales with the profit and determine which product is doing better in the market.

The pivot table feature is useful because it allows you to take in different measures, calculate and summarize them under different categories.

There are many benefits of using pivot tables, even if you do not need to compare different measures but rather use it for other purposes.

How do we use pivot tables?

In the pivot table, you specify the measure such as sales revenue, number of products etc. Then you can specify different measures for each product and get the result immediately. Then you can compare the various measures to determine where your sales are going. You can also determine the average from a few measures and compare it with the previous year's average to get an idea of how much your sales have increased.

Chapter 13. MASTERING THE DIFFERENT PARTS OF A PIVOT TABLE

There are two main components in creating Pivot tables:

- Defining fields or Field List
- Creating a table or Pivot Table Areas

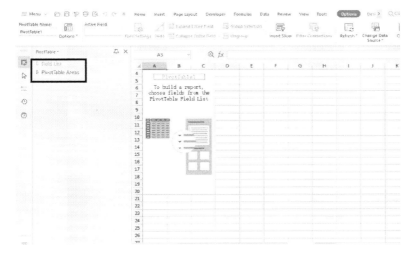

Understanding pivot tables and defining fields are important for two reasons.

1. It tells you what it is

2. It tells you how to get information into your Pivot table.

To understand this section, you need to know how Pivot tables work. The first reminder is that the Pivot table will be automatically sorted by the field that you are using, so if you choose a date field and then sort by another date field, the Pivot table will be automatically sorted by the date column.

The second thing to know is that you can define as many fields as you want for your Pivot table. This is what allows us to create a different Pivot table for each category of data, or topic.

The Pivot field list is the little icons that you see at the bottom of each column. You can tell which column is which by the little arrows on the left of the column. The Icon will change depending on what you want to do with it. You can add or delete data fields from this list by clicking the icon and dragging it up or down. If you click on the icon to highlight it, then a drop down box will appear where you can select what data that column should include in your table.

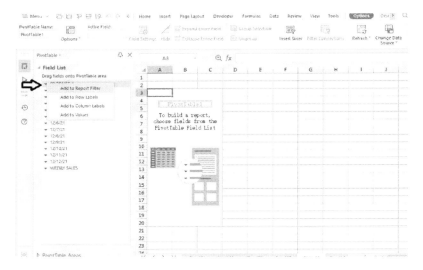

There are a couple of ways to get to the Pivot field list.

1) From a Field list column, you can click on the little arrow beside the field name.

2) You can also drag a field from the main screen to the Pivot field list.

PIVOT TABLE AREA

The Pivot table is where all the data that was selected from the Pivot field list gets put together to make a table. The Pivot table has headings for each of the categories, and where each field for that category is placed in order under those headings.

There are four parts to a Pivot table, including the Filter area, Rows, Columns and the Values.

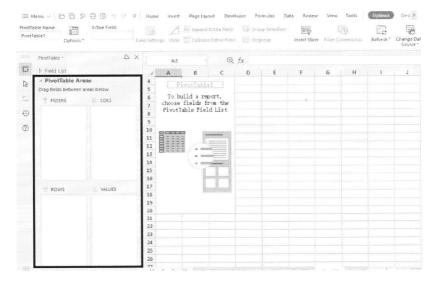

THE FILTER AREA

The filter area appears on the right-hand side of the table and it is used to apply a condition to the data. For example, clicking the Product A filter in the first pivot table allows you to select a different Product range. The formula bar at the top of Excel has a drop-down menu for automatically filtering data.

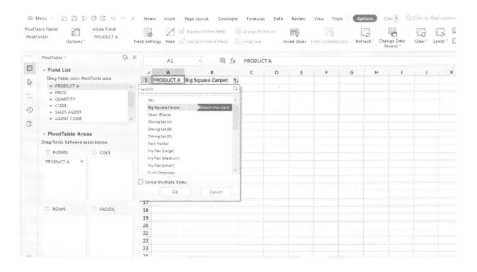

THE ROWS AREA

The Rows area of an Excel spreadsheet shows the source data from which the Pivot table has been extracted. For example, the first column in the rows area shows the names of all the Sales Agent of the Product.

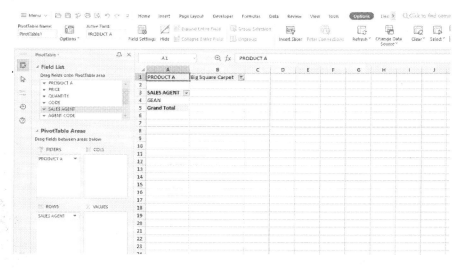

In above example, the name of "GEAN" appears under the row, it's because she's the sales agent of the said Product.

Now, let's filter the Product and select "ALL".

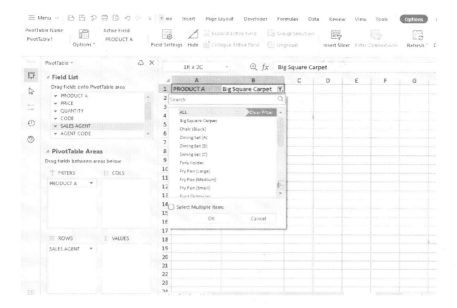

This is how it looks like:

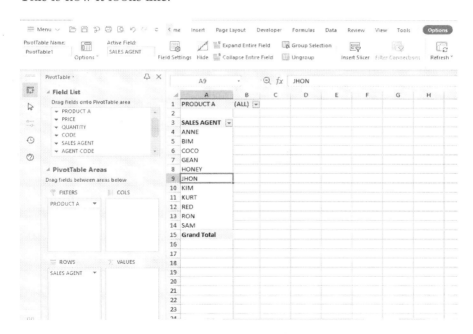

As you can see, all the name of the agents from the Product Range appears in our Pivot table. This is how to get information into your Pivot table.

THE COLUMNS AREA

The columns of the Pivot table are arranged to show the information most meaningful to you. For example, in the second pivot table, the columns are arranged to show the Sales Code.

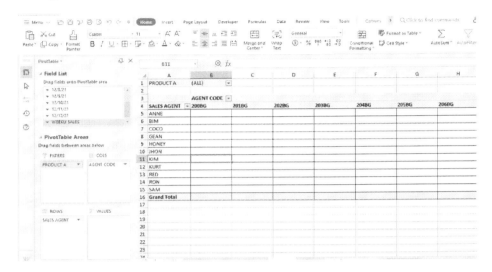

THE VALUES AREA

The Values Area is located at the bottom of a Pivot table and contains summary calculations created from the source data and can be used to further manipulate and analyze your worksheet data.

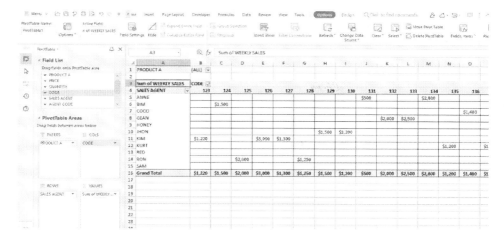

This is how your Pivot Table looks like.

USING THE COMMANDS TO ACCOMPLISH A PIVOT TABLE

Unlike with other spreadsheets, pivot tables are not limited to the dimensions of rows and columns. They can also have a value field that is split into multiple dimensions.

However, you will need to specify the settings for the value field and the value label to determine which cells in column A will be evaluated for values. To do this, open the design tab on top of your pivot table then click on value field settings symbol below fields.

You will then see the following settings:

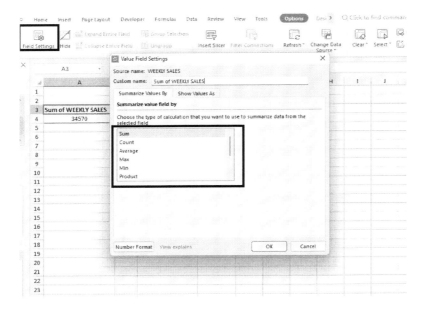

There are 11 different operations that you can choose from. Depending on your requirement, these are SUM, COUNT, AVERAGE, MAX, MIN, PRODUCT, COUNT NUMBERS, STDDEV, STDDEVP, VAR and VARP.

Sum: This operation will summarize the values in a field or column as a numerical value.

Count: This operation will count the number of values in a column or field and put it into another column.

Average: This operation will calculate the average of values from a specified row or column and place it in another cell.

Max: This operation will display the maximum value from a specified row or column and place it in another cell.

Min: This operation falls on the minimum value from a specified row or column and place it in another cell.

Product: Used to calculate the product of numbers that are found in different columns or rows, this option is selected if you want to multiply all the numbers that you have on your spreadsheet.

Count Numbers: This operation will count the number of numbers in a column or row and put into another column. This is functional if you want to display only a certain number of numbers both in your cell and on your pivot table.

STDev: is applied to calculate the standard deviation, which is a measure of how far the average value of a data set differs from the mean value.

STDVEP: This operation turns out when you have calculated the standard deviation, this will calculate the value of standard deviation and place it into another field.

VAR: This operation calculates the variance from numbers in different columns or rows, this calculation falls on the variance of the data.

VARP: This value returns the variance of numbers of the population. This is usually used in the context of being a function that is performed on a population.

What is the value field setting used for?

The main purpose of the value field setting is to extract the details that you need from all the values in a row or column. These includes:

- Summarizing data in a column or row as a whole
- Allowing you to filter out only one column or row in your pivot table
- Calculating the average and standard deviation of data in cells

The value field setting determines which operation to perform when extracting values with the extract function. There are different types of value field settings as discussed above, and we will look at all Values.

For example, you want to find how much does the Agent got on selling the product in a week. Usually, the whole table is analyzed to find out which product sold the most. Instead of searching for each one of the individual columns and rows, it's a lot easier to create a pivot table analyzing sales by each product.

To get started with it, here's what we do:

1. Make sure you have a clear data with Headings on each column and no empty rows or columns in the center of your data set and set your data is set as table.

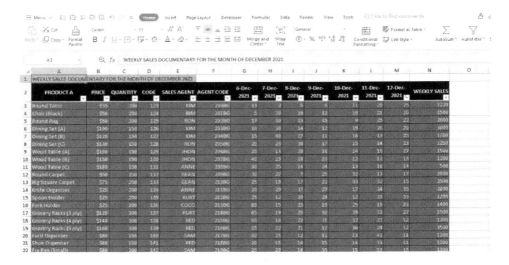

2. Rename your table so you won't get confused.

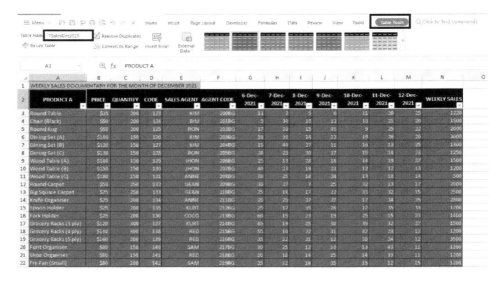

3. Go on the data tab and click Pivot Table, A window will pop up. You'll be asked to choose a location where it will be saved and then hit OK.

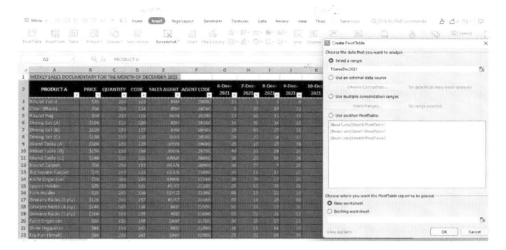

Excel will create your pivot table for you like this:

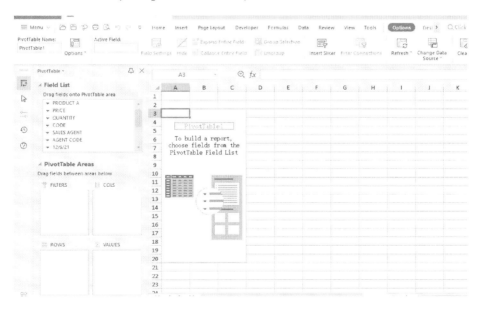

A blank pivot table appears on your worksheet. This is your work area where you will define all your fields and how they are broken down into individual items for analysis.

4. After you see your pivot table. Select any cell in the pivot table and click on Fields, you'll see a drop down list of options to organize your data set into columns.

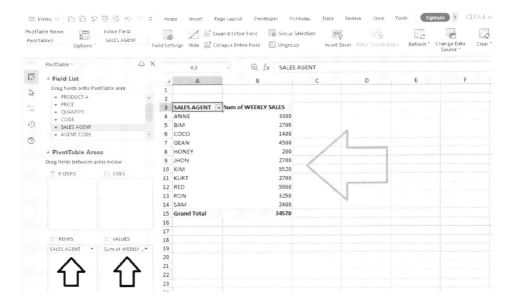

SUM VALUE

This operation will summarize the values in a field or column as a numerical value. For this example, we will set the Sales Agent in 'Row' field and Weekly Sales in 'Value' field. This is how the Sum Value Works.

Another sample using the Sum Value is to find out how many Products does the certain Agent sold for every day.

To apply this, you will need to set the data on each table. For this, let's place the Sales Agent on Filters and set the Dates in Value area.

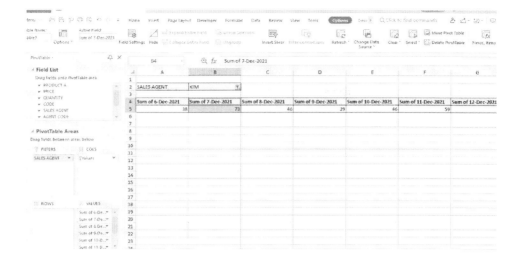

There you go, we got how many products that Agent Kim has sold every day.

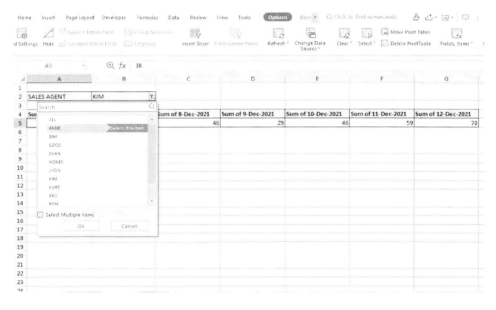

Let's check out the other agents by filtering the name. Let's choose ANNE with the products under her department.

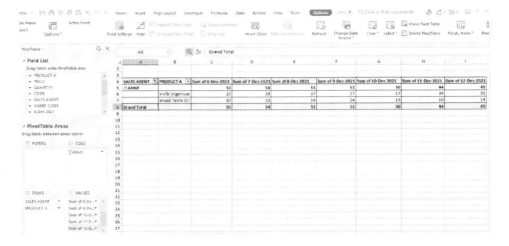

To check whether our table is correct, let's look in our data source. To do this, just double click the result value and you will be directed into a new spreadsheet showing the summarize data.

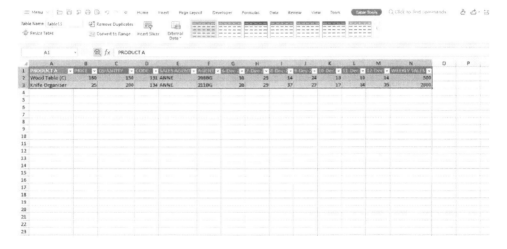

COUNT VALUE

The count operation will count the number of values in a column or field and put it into another column. For example, we have a row for sales agents, but we only want to see the total count of the products under their department.

To do this, in the Value Field Settings window, place the Product table and set the Field Settings in Count Value.

The table should look like this:

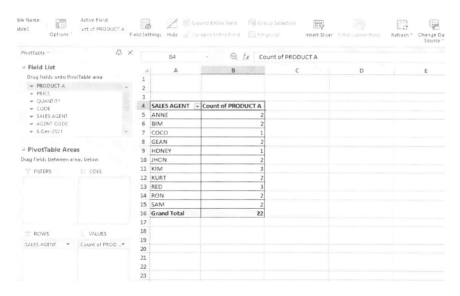

What if we would also like to know what kind of Products under their department? To do this, just simply add your Product data in Row.

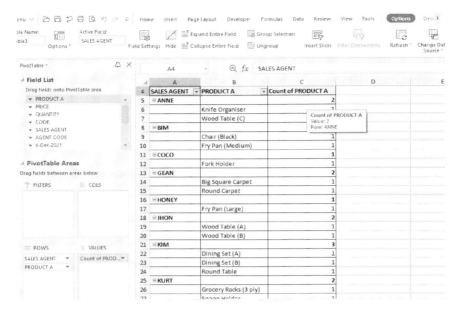

This explains that Agent Anne has two kinds of products under her department.

AVERAGE VALUE

This operation will calculate the average of values in a row or column and place it into another field. For example, the average price of each product under their department.

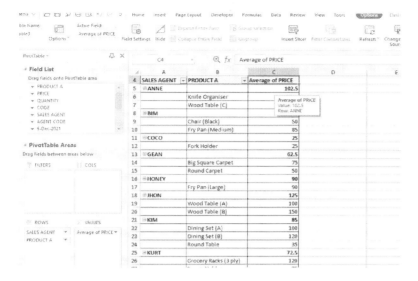

MAX VALUE

This operation will display the maximum value from a specified row or column and place it in another cell. For example, you will have a sold data for every day. The sales for each day can be calculated and recorded, but instead of adding up the numbers, we only want to see which the maximum quantity is sold value per day. You can do this by simply clicking on 'Max' value under 'Value Field Settings'. Then you will see in your pivot table that the maximum of all the sales is placed in another cell.

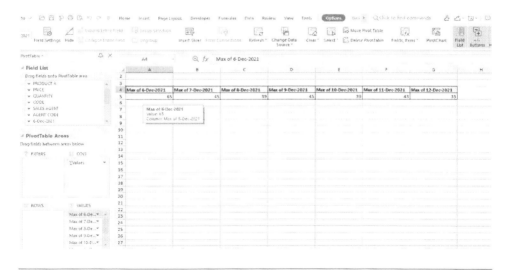

MIN VALUE

This operation falls on the minimum value from a specified row or column and place it in another cell. For example, it is the same as Max, but this time instead of displaying the maximum value from a specified row or column and place it in another cell, we want to find out the minimum value from a specified row or column and place it in another cell. We simply click on Min value under 'Value Field Settings' then our obtained data will be placed into another cell.

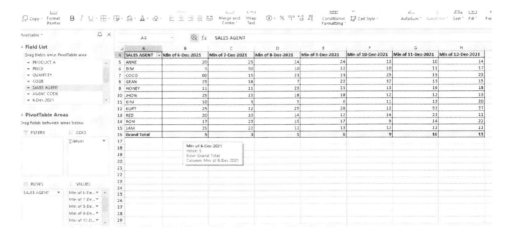

PRODUCT VALUE

This operation will calculate the product of numbers that are found in different columns or rows, this option is selected if you want to multiply all the numbers that you have on your spreadsheet.

COUNT NUMBERS VALUE

This operation will count the number of numbers in a column or row and put into another column. For example, you have one column for the product and you have a list of all salespeople assigned to each product. You can calculate the total number of salespeople from this list and put it into another column.

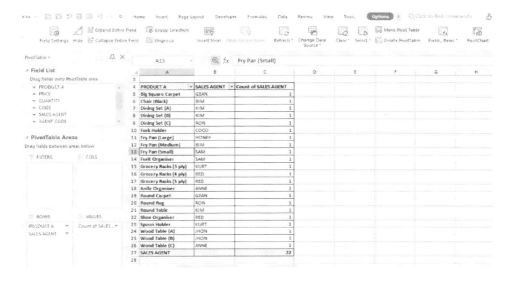

StdDev Value

StdDev is used to calculate the standard deviation, which is a measure of how far the average value of a data set differs from the mean value. In other words, it is used to test whether your numbers will be distributed normally.

For example, you have sales weekly and you want to find out the standard deviation. Firstly, calculate the average value of your weekly sales and another set of value of your weekly sales to calculate the standard deviation. Then you will see in your pivot table the result of standard deviation of your weekly sales

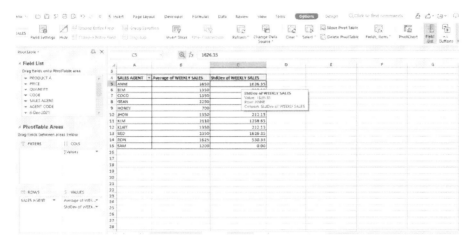

StdDevp

This operation turns out when you have calculated the standard deviation, this is an additional option that you can use to see the standard deviation on all or only some of your rows or columns.

VAR: This operation calculates the variance from numbers in different columns or rows, this calculation falls on the variance of the data. For example, you to find out the variance of your weekly sales.

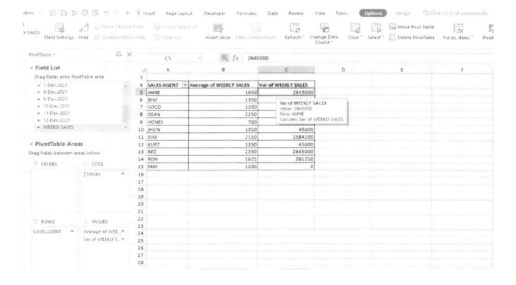

VARP VALUE

This value returns the variance of numbers of the population. This is usually used in the context of being a function that is performed on a population.

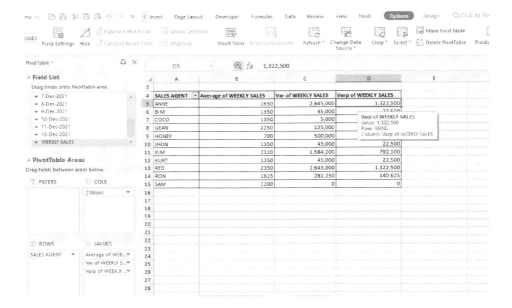

EXCEL TIPS FOR PIVOT TABLES

Here are a few Excel tips for Pivot tables that can help you get the most out of your data.

1. Be honest with yourself. If you have incomplete information, do not include that data in your pivot table. This will prevent inaccurate calculations from being done and could lead to interpretation issues later.

2. Be careful about what you include in a Pivot table. The numbers Excel looks at will change as you change what variables are included in the table.

3. Don't forget about where your data is! If your data are in a different location, then be sure to tell Excel where to find it.

4. Use a consistent column heading to help keep your Pivot table efficient. If you can, use the same naming convention for each column so that it's easier to see the relationship between them. This can be obliging if you want to export your Pivot data.

5. Don't forget about summary functions and the different options you have for them. These are great ways to simplify your numbers and help you understand what direction your business is going in.

Chapter 14. ENHANCING YOUR PIVOT TABLE PRESENTATIONS

If you're using Pivot Tables in Microsoft Excel, you'll know how important it is to make your tables as clear and concise as possible. Maximizing the effectiveness of your pivot tables is a technique that will take time and practice. We all know how important pivot tables are. A pivot table is the equivalent of a summary table that breaks down your data into one or more new columns. They can help identify trends in your data, discover patterns, simplify complicated calculations, and provide endless opportunities for exploring your data.

How to use a Subtotals option on Pivot Table

Pivot tables are great for summarizing, organizing, and analyzing data in Excel. One tool that can be used to break down your data is the SUBTOTAL function. Here's what a pivot table with subtotals looks like. It displays all the data in columns, and the subtotals for each of those data columns.

'Do not show subtotals' option on pivot tables

While the SUBTOTAL function is useful, sometimes you might not want the subtotals to be displayed in a pivot table. In this example, we won't want subtotals shown for the Sales Agent field. To do that, click the Subtotals drop down arrow, and choose `Do not show subtotals" option.

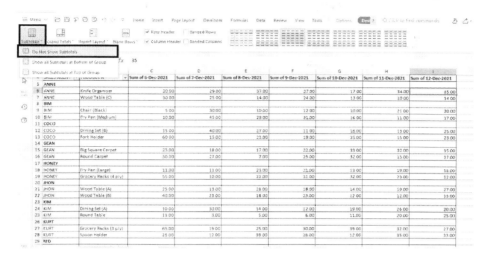

'Show Subtotal at Bottom of Group'

If you find the subtotal bar too much of an eye sore, you can hide it altogether by choosing Show Subtotal at Bottom of Group.

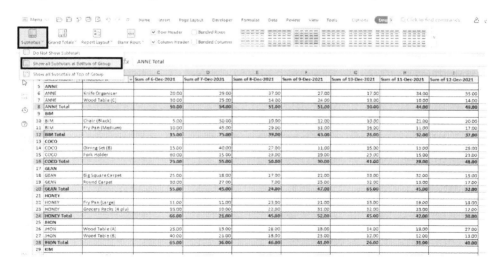

'Show Subtotal at Top of Group'

You can see the subtotal at the top of each grouping instead of putting it at the bottom.

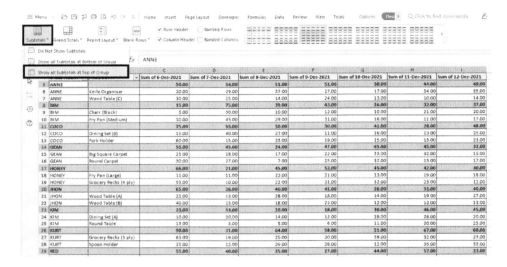

HOW TO USE GRAND TOTAL OPTION ON PIVOT TABLE

Once you have subtotals in your pivot table, you can also show grand totals. That way, it's easier to see all the data briefly.

You can hide the total by clicking 'Off for Rows and Columns' on the menu.

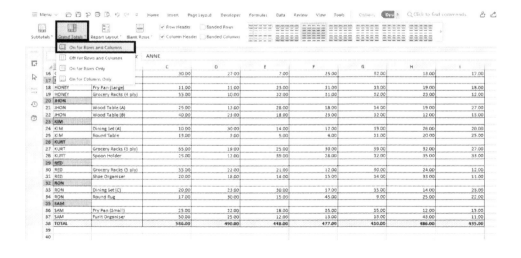

How to use Report Lay out:

The Report Layout option allows a user to change the layout format and structure of the pivot table. It consists of five sections, show in compact Form, Show in Outline Form, Show in Tabular Form, Repeat All Items Labels and Do no repeat All Item Labels.

Changing these layouts is useful when a user wants to compare data in different format or change the structure of the pivot table.

Show in compact Form

In report layout, if a user selects Show in compact form, the pivot table will be displayed in simple format. It will only show the summary and total of value items.

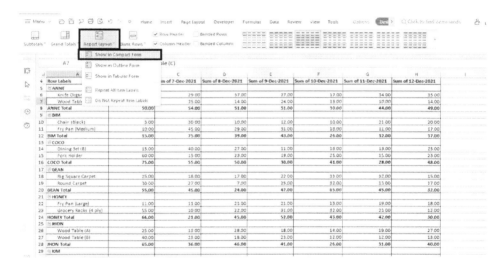

Show in outline Form

This option will display a pivot table in detailed format. It will show all the labels and values of the report in a separate column.

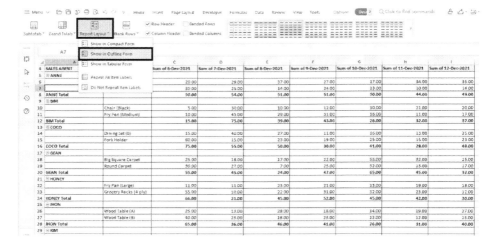

Show in tabular Form

If you want to see the pivot table in tabular format, Select this option. In tabular format, each row will be represented by a separate column, and each column will be represented by a separate row.

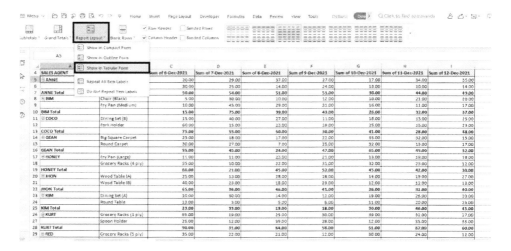

Show All Item Labels

If user want to see the item labels in the report layout, choose this option. In this case, all the items will be represented with their labels even though they are grouped under a single section.

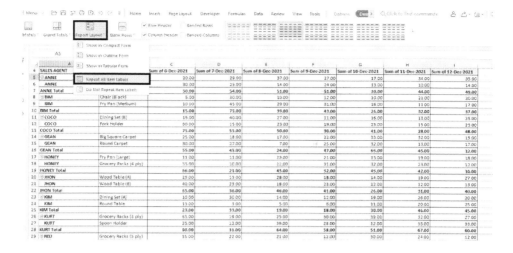

Do No Repeat Item Labels

This option is useful when a user wants to hide certain items from being repeated.

Buttons +,-

These buttons allow you to hide or show the some of the data in your field.

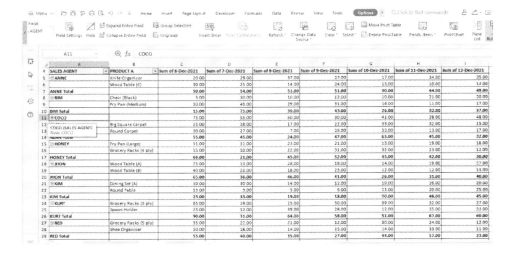

To hide this button, click on the "Options<Buttons+,-".

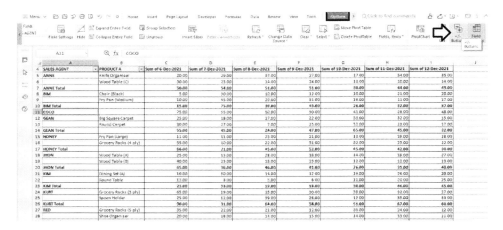

Now, you're good to go to create your Pivot Table!

PIVOT CHART AND PIVOT CHART OPTIONS

In Excel, a pivot chart is created by going to the Create tab and clicking on Pivot Chart. The options that appear depend on what is selected in the Data Field list at the top of the window.

If you have a table that summarizes your data, then you can create a pivot chart in just one step.

Pivot Charts are often used to summarize and identify trends in large data sets. They are also a very useful method for creating multiple charts from the same data set, with each chart telling a different part of the story. In the pictures below, the same table has been used to create a pivot Chart.

The main difference is that the pivot chart shows data in a more compact form and it also shows relationships between data sets in more detail.

The main reason for using a Pivot Chart over an ordinary chart is because Pivot Charts provide an interactive solution, which can be adjusted to suit your analysis needs.

Pivot charts are particularly useful when you have large amounts of data and you want to focus on parts of it.

To create a Pivot Chart, go to your table and click on the drop-down arrow at the top of the field that you want to add to your chart.

You can Create Pivot Chart from the Insert tab, which will automatically create a chart from your data. Click on the Pivot Chart, and you will see a Chart Tools. You can transform the layout of your chart, add a chart title, change your chart style and choose whether to display items in the Field List on or off. The Pivot Chart will automatically display the data in your Field List. Group headers are included with their corresponding items. If you have multiple summary levels, they will be stacked as they appear in the Field List. Excel automatically calculates a value for each member of the series where applicable.

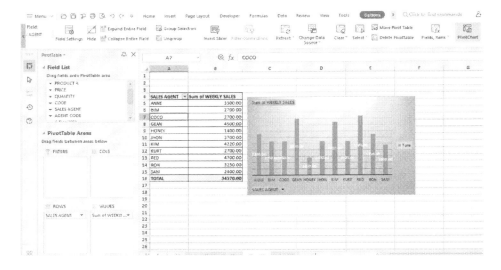

To make your Pivot Charts more effective, there are several things that you can do. For example, you could change the chart type to display the data in a different format. You may want to set a chart title or other chart elements, like legend items. You may also want to change the layout of your Pivot Chart. In incursion to changing the chart type, you can also change the field list that displays on your chart. One of the keys that you can do is change the size of the chart. You can also choose how much data to display, based on your analysis needs.

There are three standard charts that are included with Excel, which will be displayed if you press on Layout at the top of the Pivot Chart Tools. You can change the sort and layout of the chart to suit your needs. The purpose of a pivot chart is to show relationships between data. You can use pivot charts to identify trends or changes over time that are presented by changing the measure or percent columns.

INSERT SLICER

Another way that you can use with a pivot table is to create a slicer. A slicer is a row of spreadsheet cells that you can click on to drill down into the data plotted in the pivot table. You can add slicers before or after the pivot table at any location in your report. Slicers are a new way to interact with pivot table data. With slicers, you can filter and explore your data in entirely new ways.

To add slicer to the pivot table, select Insert Slicer.

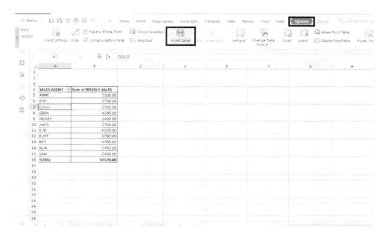

Now enter the values of slicer in the combo box then click OK button.

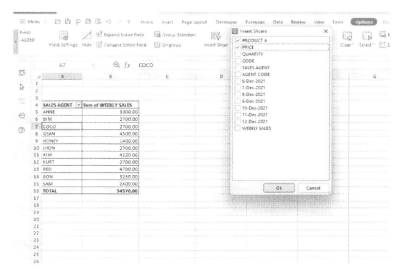

A new button will appear with name of selected pivot table on it.

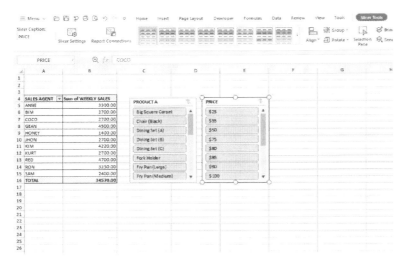

Now you can use these columns as if it is an additional data column in your pivot table.

SELECTION PANE

Selection pane allows you to find or hide a single object in the pivot table. In this case, if you select an item and you want to hide it, select selection pane and click on Hide Button.

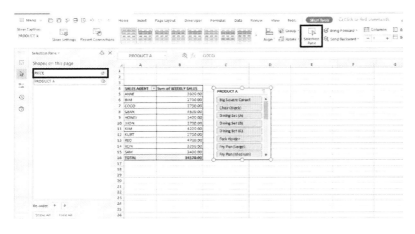

Slicer allows you to easily find the data you are looking for without having to scroll through the pivot table.

For example, if you want to find data which is related with the product, you can click the data and it will automatically show the result.

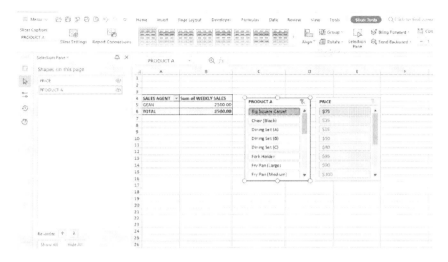

This shows the price and the Sales Agent of the said product.

Often, your pivot table will be summarizing what other options were chosen by different individuals, so you'll want to customize the table with colors or icons reflecting these selections.

Still, while Pivot Tables offer an enormous amount of power and functionality, sometimes simple enhancements make things even easier for you.

Chapter 15.   GETTING TO KNOW FORMULAS

Formulas are the heart of Excel. You should learn how to write formulas that do calculations, combine values, and refer to cells in your spreadsheet.

Types of Formulas

Excel provides three types of calculation formulas: arithmetic, financial, and look-up. Each of these formulas is defined with a particular function key.

ARITHMETIC FORMULAS

Arithmetic formulas are used to perform calculations and determine the results of mathematical operations with numbers. The most common arithmetic formulas you will use in Excel are simple math functions and common arithmetic operators (such as +, -, *, /). You can also find these functions in your word processor's calculator.

FINANCIAL FORMULAS

Financial formulas calculate financial transactions using money values, such as interest rates and percentages. To learn how to write financial formulas in Excel, you will need to know how to use some financial formulas in formulas that operate with these values.

LOOK-UP FORMULAS

Look-up formulas are used to find information, such as the size or year of a company's financial statement or the cost of gasoline in 5 different states. The most common look-up formulas you will use in Excel are INDEX, MATCH, and IFERROR. These functions determine the results of locating data in a range or table.

How to Work with Formulas

You can place a formula into a cell by typing it or by copying it from another cell. These steps will show you how to enter data in a cell, including entering formulas.

1. Enter data in a cell by typing.
2. To enter a formula, click in the cell, and then type = (equal sign).
3. In the formula bar, type the formula's components (arguments), such as values and operators.
4. Press "Enter" to finish.
5. To see your formula result in the cell, go to the cell and click "Formula." The Formula bar displays your formula and its result.

Before you learn how to write formulas, you should be aware of the following things:

DEFINING FUNCTIONS IN EXCEL

A function is a set of instructions that performs a calculation or an action on the values in a cell. The formula enclosed in parentheses is called an argument. A function can obtain any number of arguments, but the number and types of these arguments depend on the function.

In Excel, you can create two types of functions: User-defined (formulas) and built-in (built-in functions).

USER-DEFINED FUNCTIONS

A user-defined function is a piece of programming code that you create. You write the code in Visual Basic for Applications (VBA), which is the programming language for Excel and other Office applications. Then, you run the VBA macro to see the results of your function in the worksheet.

Built-in functions are formulas that come with Excel and perform a variety of actions on cells. Most of them are simple mathematical formulas, but some of them perform more complex tasks, such as looking up data in a table.

Built-in functions have the following characteristics:

- They can be used in any worksheet.
- They are easy to use and understand.
- They are portable from one workbook to another.
- They have "built-in" error checking, so if you make an error in your function, Excel displays an alert dialog box and stops executing the function.
- You cannot create any new built-in functions in Excel. You can only use the ones that are available or add them to a custom toolbar later.
- They are named by the first letters of the function.
- They generally perform the same actions in all Excel versions.
- They use a set of arguments that you specify and may have functions that return values.
- Depending on the type of function, you can use one or more arguments.

UNDERSTANDING ARGUMENTS

The arguments for a function are the values you put inside the parentheses in a formula. The arguments are used by the function to calculate its results. You must specify all the required arguments when you create a function, but you can usually leave empty any optional arguments that you do not need.

Example of arguments:

=sum(A1:B10)

=Sum(Number1, ...)

In the formula above, the arguments are used as follows:

Number1 - this argument is the input range, which can be an array formula. For example, if you want to sum cells A1 through A10, you will input =sum(A1:A10). These arguments are the other input ranges for your formula.

The output will be a single cell with the value of each range (the sum of column C) added together (sum of B column).

=Date(year,month,date)

In the formula above, the first argument is the date to find, and the second argument is the year, month, and date.

=FV(rate, nper, pmt, pv, [fnce])

In the formula above, the following arguments are specified: rate — this argument is used to set the interest rate for this payment. nper — this argument sets the number of payments. pmt — this argument is used to set the amount of each payment. pv —this argument sets the current unpaid balance. [fnce] – if you do not specify an optional argument, you must use brackets ([]) to indicate that it is an optional one.

=if(logical_test,value_if_true,[value_if_false])

In the formula above, the following arguments are:

x: The result of the logical test can be either "true" or "false."

value_if_x: The value the formula returns when the variable x is true. If it evaluates to false, then that argument will not appear in the formula.

#N/A: This means that there is no such value for this argument.

REASONS FOR USING FORMULAS IN EXCEL

There are various reasons why you will use formulas in Excel. The first reason is that doing so enables you to see the results of a calculation or an action on your worksheet. This can help you make better-informed decisions and control the actions in your worksheet.

The second reason is that you might want to perform calculations with variables, such as the number of sales or the daily sales so that you can change these numbers without having to change all your formulas.

The third reason is that performing calculations can help you manage multiple worksheets in a workbook. For instance, in a business bookkeeping application, you might need to enter data for your vendors, customers, and employees. If you do this in one worksheet, you need to check and update that data in all the other worksheets. By using functions, you can easily update those values after entering data into the first worksheet, and all the other customer, sales, and employee records will be updated automatically.

The fourth reason is if you want to make up your own functions by using a variety of Excel features by combining different parts of Excel. For example, you can form an Excel formula to perform a calculation on the New Year's date and to create a custom date field in your worksheet.

The fifth reason is that even if you do not use formulas in Excel, every time you save your workbook, the workbook displays formulas and comments, which are helpful for program writers and document maintainers.

IMPORTANT THINGS TO KNOW ABOUT FUNCTIONS

There are five important things that I want to share with you:

1. Functions can be very long, so be careful about what you enter in the cell. The function enclosed in parentheses is called the function's argument or argument. For example, the formula =COUNTA(A:B:D) refers to the range A:B:D.

2. Functions can also include text (words). If you select a cell that contains the formula and then copy it to another cell, Excel pastes that text instead of replacing it with numbers within the formula.

3. If you create a formula with incorrect spelling or syntax, Excel displays a #NAME? error in the cell. The formula works only when you correct the error.

4. The question mark (?) is called a wildcard because it represents any value. When Excel replaces the question mark with a value, it performs calculations on that value according to what you specified in your function formula.

5. If you press F4 on a cell that contains a formula, Excel displays the results of your function and its arguments. This is called "displaying the formula." You can also press F4 to display information about your function in the formula bar.

Chapter 16. FORMULAS

As you may already know, Excel is the most popular spreadsheet application out there. It's used by a vast majority of companies, universities, and individuals. Its flexibility has allowed it to become one of the most widely-used applications in the world. Therefore, many users call for help when they need to insert formulas into their spreadsheets to get an output or manipulate data.

As a spreadsheet application, Excel also allows you to create formulas and use functions that can be used to compute new values for cells. Using these tools, you can efficiently perform complex calculations such as calculating averages, sums, or different types of statistics. Also, using functions, you can write formulas that combine other inputs with the result being displayed in one cell. This part will give you a glimpse of these features and how they can help in the work you do.

Excel also allows you to work further with your work data by using various formatting options. These include using multiple colors, fonts, and borders to make your results look more impressive.

Instead of using formulas, you can also enter arithmetic operations in cells via functions.

The result is displayed in another cell, which is known as the referencing cell (C2 in this case).

Let's look at an example when we want to calculate the age of all employees in our database. First, you would need to create a table: NAME AND DATE OF BIRTH. Our formula is simply:

=datedif(b2,today(),"Y") , in this formula , the letter "Y" stands for how many years old the person is.

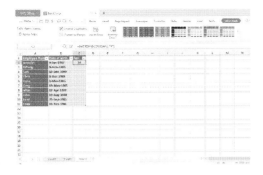

Excel is not an easy program for beginners to learn and can average out to be quite confusing and difficult. However, it is still a good program that is widely used across the globe and has many benefits.

IF-formula in excel is a formula that you can use to calculate the value of an investment at any given point, which is useful when calculating profit or loss.

This formula is one of the most important formulas to learn in excel because it's used everywhere and it will allow you to calculate profit or loss at any point. To test if a cell is not blank, you use the "not equal to" operator (<>) in combination with an empty string (""). As the result if cell C2 is not empty, the formula returns "Yes", otherwise "No":

You'll learn a simple and most common formula in Excel that is often overlooked by most people who learn the program.

Most common formulas in excel

SUM

=SUM(D3:D14)

Calculates the total of cells D3 through D14

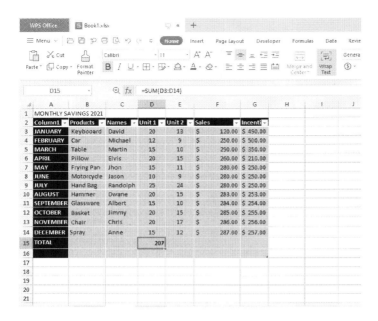

This formula is common to use when summing up a range of cells.

=SUM(D3, E14)

Adds up values in cells D3 and E14

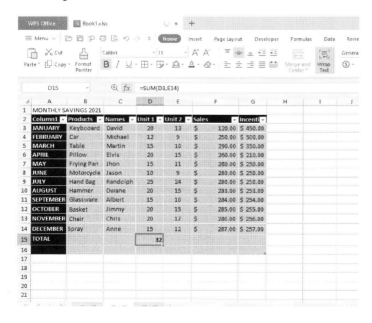

This formula will calculate the total of the values in cells B2 and B6.

AVERAGE

=AVERAGE(B2:B21)

Use this formula to calculate the average.

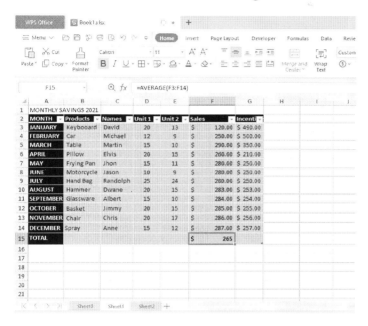

This formula is the most used in Excel.

This sample shows you the total Average of students on their scores using the formula:

=AVERAGE(B2:D2)

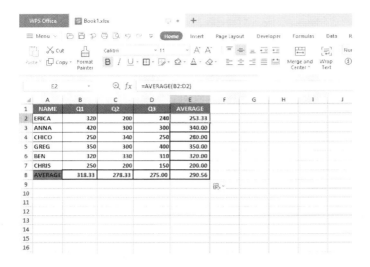

MATCH

=MATCH(I5,B3:B7,0)

The Match function will find the position of a certain value in a list and return the relative position number.

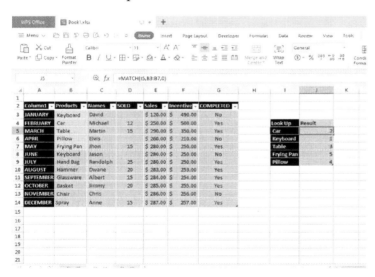

This is very useful when you must match information from different locations and you do not know where exactly this information will be.

SUBTOTAL

=SUBTOTAL(1,D3:D14)

The SUBTOTAL() function is one of the most commonly used formulas in Excel. SUBTOTAL() function calculates the total of a range of cells. Depending on what you want, you can select average, count, sum, min, max, min, and others.

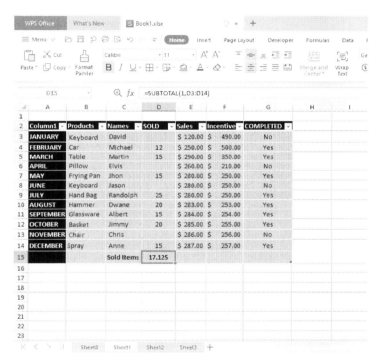

The subtotal calculation on cells ranging from D3 to D14 and in the subtotal list "1" refers to average. This can be exceptionally helpful when creating formulas and performing calculations

IF FUNCTION

The IF function is the most common formula in Excel. You can use it to create a table or chart with changing values.

=COUNTIF(E3:E14,15)

131

Use this formula to count the number of cells containing the number 15.

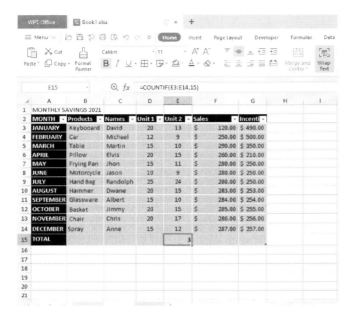

This is useful for calculating frequency distributions.

=SUMIF(B3:B14,I3,D3:D14)

This formula will add up all the values in a table where a condition is met.

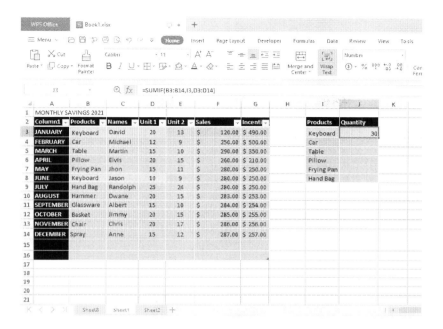

Counts the number of times "I3" appears in cells D3:D14. The formula outputs the value 30 when "I3" is included in D3 to D14 and 0 otherwise.

=IF(D3<>"","Yes","No")

This formula can be used to calculate the answer of yes or no when a condition is met.

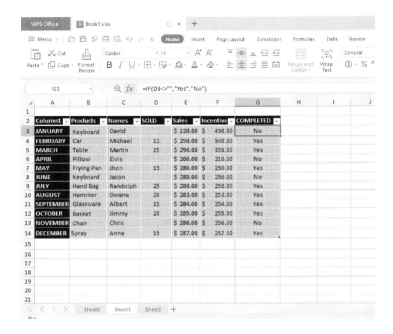

It's very useful when you have several conditions in which you must check whether a certain result has been met or not.

TRIM FUNCTION

Trim Function removes all the characters from a string and places them in front of itself.

=Trim(A2)

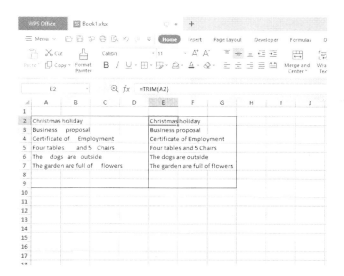

Takes no arguments and will remove all spaces from both ends of a string.

MAX AND MIN

This formula can be used to find the maximum or minimum value of a given range. Let's say you want to find the highest incentives in a list using this formula:

=MAX(F3:F14)

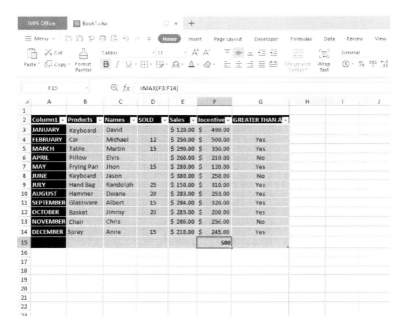

And let's find out the lowest incentives in a list using this formula:

=MIN(F3:F14)

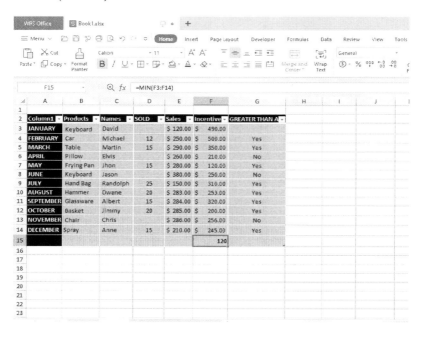

This is very useful to find the highest and lowest value in a list that may exceed the maximum number allowed.

DATE AND TIME FUNCTION

The current date and time can also be determined with two formulas: =NOW() or =TODAY(). Today and now functions can be found in any version of Microsoft Excel. The most common formula is =TODAY(), which displays the date for today.

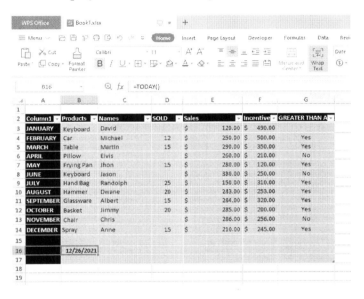

The second most common formula is =NOW(), which displays the date and time for now.

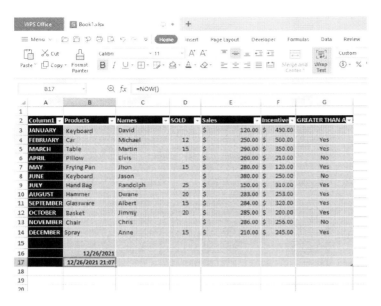

The date and time functions in Excel can be used for a variety of purposes including calculating an employee's work hours, the amount of time until a project is due, or calculating the number of days since your last meeting. Some functions that can be used to calculate the number of days between two dates are DATEDIF, DATEDIF2, DATEVALUE and WORKDAY.

The TIME function can be used to return or calculate any type of time values in Excel, including hours, minutes, seconds and so on. It can also return formatted time values in letters like AM/PM words.

=TIME(B2,C2,D2)

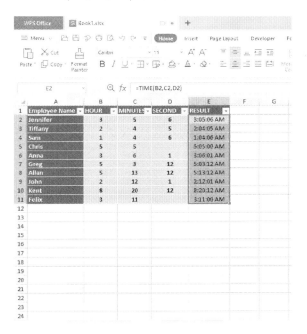

Calculating an employees pay for a day, a month or a year is easy by using the TIME function.

Another example to calculate the time that the employee worked an 8 hours shift is one of the very common formulas in excel. The formula in excel for calculating the hours worked is as follows:

=(C2-B2)*24

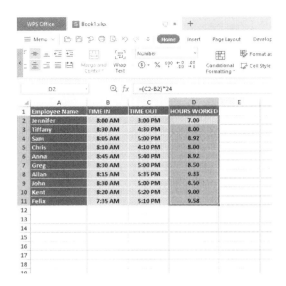

We used the decimal 24 in this formula because the decimal 24 is a factor of 60 minutes and 60 minutes is equal to 1 hour.

Another example is calculating time difference between two date/times from two columns in Excel. This function is very useful to calculate how long it will take to deliver some work at the client site and a lot of other examples where you want to calculate the time.

It is a very common formula in excel,

=TEXT(C2-B2,"HH:MM:SS")

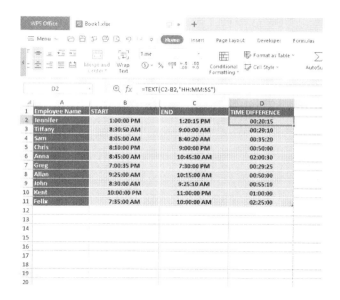

When we give the formula for calculating time difference above, we must write "HH:MM:SS", for hour, minute and second.

Now, we want to know if the employee has delivered the project in 30 minutes or has crossed in 30 minutes.

We will use the IF function, which will return CROSSED or WITHIN to say if the employee has done the job within 30 minutes or not.

=IF(HOUR(D2)>0,"Crossed",IF(MINUTE(D2)>30,"Crossed",IF(AND(MINUTE(D2)=30,SECOND(D2)>0,"Crossed","Within")))

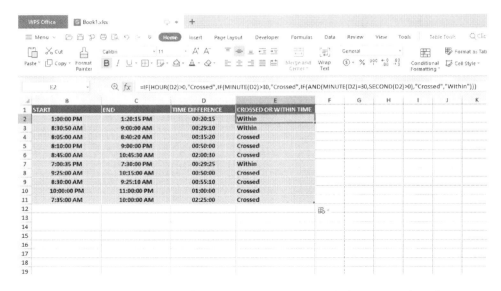

We know that the result in first column is WITHIN, it means that the project has been completed within 30 minutes and for other result is CROSSED, it means the project has taken more than 30 minutes.

VPLOOKUP

You've created the perfect spreadsheet with all sorts of formulas to calculate your net pay. You want to include this formula into your spreadsheet, but you're not sure how.

The VLOOKUP function is a helpful function to use, if you want to search an array of data and return a result that matches your criteria.

The VLOOKUP function serves 2 purposes:

For example, let's say you have a list of information about your employees and their salaries. You can use the VLOOKUP function to retrieve their net pay. The formula is:

=VLOOKUP(G3,A2:D9,4,FALSE)

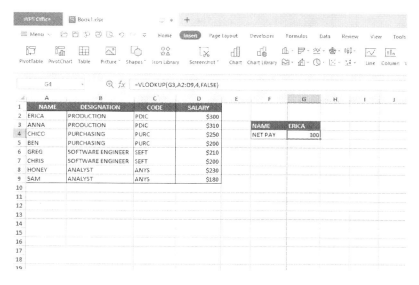

Using the VLOOKUP function is a very simple formula. It's as follows:
=VLOOKUP(lookup_value,table_array,index_num,match_type)

The formula above gives you the result. Notice that if the lookup value is not found in the table into which you are trying to look up, then Null returns its value.

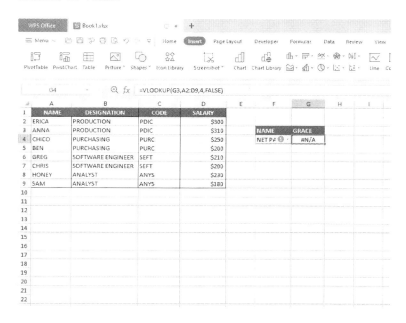

An alternative to the VLOOKUP is the HLOOKUP function. The HLOOKUP performs a similar function to the VLOOKUP, except that it works horizontally instead of vertically.

Hence, the HLOOKUP function searches from left to right and returns a result based on your specified criteria.

The formula is:
=HLOOKUP(lookup_value,table_array,row_num,column_num). The three parameters in this formula are:

1. Lookup value- the value you are searching for in the corresponding cell (C2 or 567).
2. Table Array- where the data is located (A2:D4).
3. Row- number you are searching from (3).
4. False- indicates to an exact match
5. True- indicates an approximate match

For example, if you want to find the total of the column A (for instance, employee code) and the row 3 (for instance, value for employee salary), your formula should look like this: =HLOOKUP(567,A2:D4,3,FALSE)

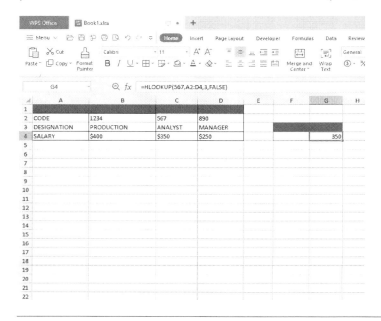

That's all you must do to create and use a spreadsheet formula.

INDEX

The index formula is an indispensable tool that can be used throughout Excel when working on tables, charts, or graphs. It really becomes invaluable when combined with other formulas such as MATCH, MIN and MAX functions. The index formula is a versatile tool that can be used in many different situations and can be used to solve problems quickly.

The first example is one that can be done with any type of table. The goal of this formula is to identify what month an employee was hired in. By doing this you will be able to restructure the table and have a more refined profile of each employee. In the first column of the table, you can identify the name of each employee. Then in the second column, you can identify which month they were hired and so on.

The formula is as follows:

=INDEX(B2:B17,MATCH(J3,A2:A17,0))

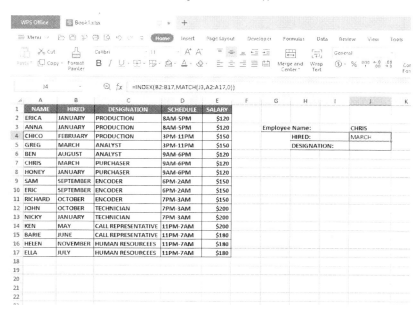

The parameters: =INDEX(array,
MATCH(lookup_value,lookup_array,[Match_type])

The formula starts by verifying that you are in the correct column. The next step is to get the correct row for your data point. The formula MATCH(J3,A2:A17,0) does this. It finds index J3 in column A and then locates the corresponding value in column A (the second parameter) at row 2 (the first parameter). The last piece of this INDEX formula is to verify that it returned a blank cell if no match was found. This is indicated with zero (0).

This next example is locating the designation of each employee.

The formula goes with:

=INDEX(C2:C17,MATCH(J3,A2:A17,0))

In the images above, we can see how this formula was used to restructure the spreadsheet. We can see that the table is significantly more refined down to two specific employees. An additional benefit of using this formula is that you will be able to identify employees in different tables. This is great for keeping track of all employees and who they are.

Chapter 17. VARIOUS FORMULAS

Excel is a powerful program that has been used in the workplace since 1989. This part will show you how to quickly access, view and use various formula in Excel. They may be used in simple financial models, calculations for work or school projects and other accounting tasks. The formulas may also be used to showcase data created by a spreadsheet application or another program. It allows users to perform almost any type of task, from creating graphs, to calculating interest on loans or making business models. One of the most useful formulas in Excel is the formula for determining taxes if you are planning on doing an accountancy course and are uncertain what calculators might be necessary. There are two types of taxes in Excel: Pay as you go tax and Pre-tax tax. The first, pay as you go Tax, is only available for companies with a single employee. The Pre-tax tax, however, can be used for any type of company or business.

The pre-tax tax uses the following formula: =B2+D2 which will tell you how much money should be contributed to taxes each period. You can group similar calculations into a single cell with the use of a parenthesis "()" or "(", so that the calculations can be simplified. The sum must be made separately by each part of the calculation to determine your overall income, any deductions and tax amount.

	A	B	C	D	E	F	G	H	I
1	NAME	SALARY	TAX RATE	TAXES	TOTAL				
2	ERICA	$200.00	5.09%	$10	$210.18				
3	ANNA	$250.00	5.09%	$13	$262.73				
4	CHICO	$280.00	5.09%	$14	$294.25				
5	GREG	$300.00	5.09%	$15	$315.27				
6	BEN	$350.00	5.09%	$18	$367.82				
7	CHRIS	$300.00	5.09%	$15	$315.27				
8	HONEY	$330.00	5.09%	$17	$346.80				
9	SAM	$320.00	5.09%	$16	$336.29				
10	ERIC	$450.00	5.09%	$23	$472.91				
11	RICHARD	$430.00	5.09%	$22	$451.89				
12	JOHN	$420.00	5.09%	$21	$441.38				
13	NICKY	$410.00	5.09%	$21	$430.87				
14	KEN	$380.00	5.09%	$19	$399.34				
15	BARIE	$350.00	5.09%	$18	$367.82				
16	HELEN	$320.00	5.09%	$16	$336.29				
17	ELLA	$330.00	5.09%	$17	$346.80				
18									

There are two different methods used to calculate one's own income: Gross Income Method and Net Income Method. The Gross Income Method uses the formula: =SUM(B2:D2) where B is Your Base Salary and C is Your Allowance and D is your bonus. It is also recommended that your employer allows for the deduction of a certain sum from the pay, whether it be for health insurance, or for education. This option is available at the end of the tax calculator and will appear as a separate line item under your pay. It is advisable that you use this option if you know that wages have already been taxed at the employer level.

	A	B	C	D	E	F	G
1	NAME	SALARY	ALLOWANCE	BONUS	TOTAL		
2	ERICA	$200.00	$10.00	$100	$310.00		
3	ANNA	$250.00	$10.00	$100	$360.00		
4	CHICO	$280.00	$10.00	$100	$390.00		
5	GREG	$300.00	$10.00	$100	$410.00		
6	BEN	$350.00	$10.00	$100	$460.00		
7	CHRIS	$300.00	$10.00	$100	$410.00		
8	HONEY	$330.00	$10.00	$100	$440.00		
9	SAM	$320.00	$10.00	$100	$430.00		
10	ERIC	$450.00	$10.00	$100	$560.00		
11	RICHARD	$430.00	$10.00	$100	$540.00		
12	JOHN	$420.00	$10.00	$100	$530.00		
13	NICKY	$410.00	$10.00	$100	$520.00		
14	KEN	$380.00	$10.00	$100	$490.00		
15	BARIE	$350.00	$10.00	$100	$460.00		
16	HELEN	$320.00	$10.00	$100	$430.00		
17	ELLA	$430.00	$10.00	$100	$440.00		
18							
19							
20							
21							
22							
23							

The second method, Net Income Method, uses the formula: =E3-F3-G3-H3-I3 where E is Your Total Gross Income Salary which will be deducted into your tax, health insurance, car insurance and savings. This formula is slightly more complex than the previous one but is a little less complicated to understand. The advantage of doing this calculation over the first one is that it takes into consideration any possible tax deductions or bonuses, which are not considered by other calculation methods.

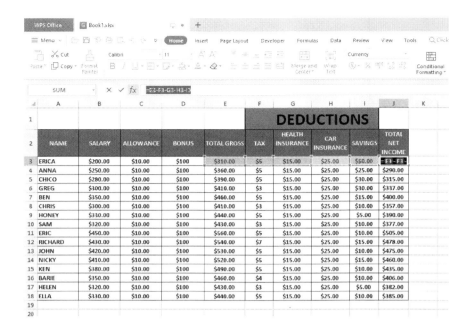

	A	B	C	D	E	F	G	H	I	J	K
1							**DEDUCTIONS**				
2	NAME	SALARY	ALLOWANCE	BONUS	TOTAL GROSS	TAX	HEALTH INSURANCE	CAR INSURANCE	SAVINGS	TOTAL NET INCOME	
3	ERICA	$200.00	$10.00	$100	$310.00	$5	$15.00	$25.00	$50.00	=E3-F3-	
4	ANNA	$250.00	$10.00	$100	$360.00	$5	$15.00	$25.00	$25.00	$290.00	
5	CHICO	$280.00	$10.00	$100	$390.00	$5	$15.00	$25.00	$30.00	$315.00	
6	GREG	$300.00	$10.00	$100	$410.00	$3	$15.00	$25.00	$30.00	$337.00	
7	BEN	$350.00	$10.00	$100	$460.00	$5	$15.00	$25.00	$15.00	$400.00	
8	CHRIS	$300.00	$10.00	$100	$410.00	$3	$15.00	$25.00	$10.00	$357.00	
9	HONEY	$330.00	$10.00	$100	$440.00	$5	$15.00	$25.00	$5.00	$390.00	
10	SAM	$320.00	$10.00	$100	$430.00	$3	$15.00	$25.00	$10.00	$377.00	
11	ERIC	$450.00	$10.00	$100	$560.00	$5	$15.00	$25.00	$10.00	$505.00	
12	RICHARD	$430.00	$10.00	$100	$540.00	$7	$15.00	$25.00	$15.00	$478.00	
13	JOHN	$420.00	$10.00	$100	$530.00	$5	$15.00	$25.00	$10.00	$475.00	
14	NICKY	$410.00	$10.00	$100	$520.00	$5	$15.00	$25.00	$15.00	$460.00	
15	KEN	$380.00	$10.00	$100	$490.00	$5	$15.00	$25.00	$10.00	$435.00	
16	BARIE	$350.00	$10.00	$100	$460.00	$4	$15.00	$25.00	$10.00	$406.00	
17	HELEN	$320.00	$10.00	$100	$430.00	$3	$15.00	$25.00	$5.00	$382.00	
18	ELLA	$330.00	$10.00	$100	$440.00	$5	$15.00	$25.00	$10.00	$385.00	
19											
20											

PRESENT VALUE FUNCTION

PV function returns the present value of an investment based on constant annual payments and an interest rate. The formula has three parameters: the rate, the number of payments (NPER) and the payment made (PMT).

To calculate PV in Excel, enter the following into cell:

=PV(C2,C3,C4,0)

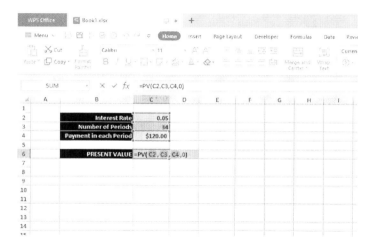

The PMT parameter is useful since it allows you to change the number of payments made throughout your project so that you can see how much your present value calculation changes over time. The NPER parameter, is the number of payments that are made. The formula will return a positive or negative value between 0 and 1, depending on whether there are more payments to be made or not. The main part of this function is to answer a question about how much you should invest today to be able to save enough money for a future purchase.

FUTURE FUNCTION

The FV Function returns the future value of money in one lump sum with payments and interest received in a series of time periods. This function is valuable for planning purposes and solving business problems. Here is the syntax for the FV Function:

FV(rate, nper, pmt, pv, [fnce])

The FV Function takes six arguments. The Rate argument refers to the percent interest rate per period ([0,1] or 0%). The Nper argument that refers to the number of payment periods (note: periods must be > 0). The Pmt argument that refers to the payment made each period and has a corresponding sign (+ or -). The PV argument refers to present value.

Example, you had loan $1,000 at 10% interest rate. $50 is paid every month for 1 year. How much will you pay for that loan? Let's take an example to understand it:

Let's look at below formula:

=FV(C5/12,C6*12,C4,C3)

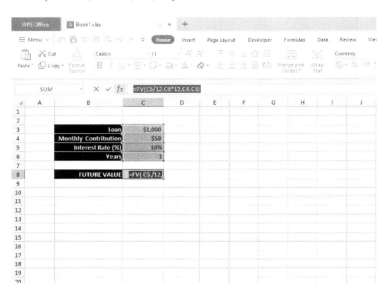

In the formula above, the FV Function calculates future value of $1,000 borrowed at 10% interest rate which divide into 12 (months) for 1 year payment multiply into 12 (months) with $50 payment every month. In other words, it calculates amount we need to pay for that loan. The formula returns ($1,732.99).

STANDARD DEVIATION

Another example is the calculation of the standard deviation.

The standard deviation is how far from the mean a collection of data can vary. This is important to know, because it shows how many of the values in a set are more or less than some given value. For example, if you took a test and got an 80% score, your standard deviation would be 0 (because your score was included twice on the scale). If you took a test and got 85%, however, your standard deviation would be 1 (because only one out of all those numbers was greater than 85%).

This is a measure used in statistics to describe how much an individual data point varies from the mean - it's a squared difference from it with positive or negative signs.

The standard deviation of a set of data is the data standard deviation divided by the square root of the total number of data points. Standard deviation is widely used in business and finance, especially in statistical analysis and portfolio management. It is also used in computer science to calculate numeric properties or to compare one thing with another, such as price to value ratio (P/V).

To see how this works with an example, let's suppose you have data from a male and female biceps curl experiment, where you measured the biceps curl power in lbs. and recorded them in sheet 1 of an Excel file.

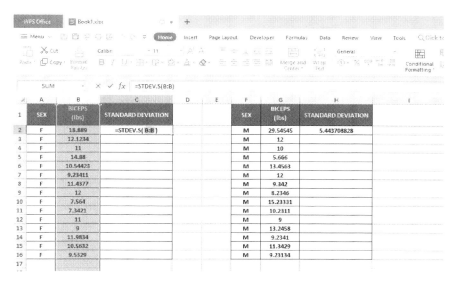

This formula uses this piece of data, which was collected from a biceps curl experiment you ran.

If you look at the formula, you'll see that it computes the standard deviation based on the data quantity as well as the number of samples. The formula returns a decimal number so that it can be used in Excel calculations.

Chapter 18. TRACING FUNCTIONALITY

We'll be focusing on how to trace functionality in Excel. There are several ways to do this, but we'll be going over the most common method. We'll also explore a few of the benefits that you can get from tracing functionality in Excel. It's important to note that there are many good reasons for doing so, including being able to track changes in formulas, uncovering errors in workbooks and getting rid of manual dependencies. Without further ado, let's get started!

One of the most important skills you can learn in Excel is how to trace functionality. This skill will provide you with an invaluable tool for troubleshooting and research. The first step to learning this skill is understanding what functions are exactly. And as you might know, there are three types: basic, input, and output. It is beneficial to learn as much as you can about each function to master this skill.

Functions are a way to take numerical, logical, text and even cell references in your worksheet, and apply them to your data set. Often you may use multiple functions in the same worksheet at the same time. For example: You might want to sum the values in column B by both minimum and maximum. And you want that these two calculations be done within a loop so you can run through the values many times.

INPUT FUNCTIONS

We will first talk about input functions. These functions require something to be input into the function for it to return a result. For example, if you had a list of homework assignments and they were in no order, you could use the IF function to determine which assignment is due next based on the number of assignments completed. Or you may use something like NOW to show the current date and time. Or using TODAY to show just today's date.

OUTPUT FUNCTIONS

output functions are the opposite of input functions, they don't require something to be entered into them. Instead, they return a result based on the information they have been given. For example, the SUM function will take values and add them up, but it will not tell you what the final value is. You would then use something like IF, TODAY, or TODAYIF to get that answer for us.

BASIC FUNCTIONS

Basic functions are normally the ones you will use most often. These are the kind of functions that take in a cell or range of cells, look at that value and return a result. For example, if you had grades for each student, and wanted to find the average grade for all the students, you could simply use AVERAGE. Or if we had a list of numbers we wanted to multiply together. We could use PRODUCT to multiply them all together and then divide by how many numbers we put into it. Basic functions are the ones that are most important for the goal we are trying to accomplish in our worksheet.

INPUT VS. OUTPUT:

This is one of the most important things to note, when you are using a basic function, it completely depends on what you feed it. For the function to return a result, you must input something in. If you do not input anything, then the function cannot return a result. But if you do input something into it, then the function will return that result. If your function requires nothing to be input, then it is classified as an output function. Enjoy!

OUTPUT VS. INPUT:

This is also a very important thing to note, just because we are outputting a result does not mean everything you put into the formula will be returned as a result. For the function to return a result, you will need to input something in. A basic example of this is when we are doing subtraction in our worksheet. When we must do a subtraction, we must input something in, which is the number on the left side of the equals sign. For example, if I wanted to subtract 10 from 50, I would type in -10, not 10 into the cell. If you do not input something in it will give you an error message.

TRACING FORMULAS

Tracing Functionality in excel involves figuring out where a formula is coming from. If a formula is coming from another cell or cells, it would be considered Cell Reference or Named Range. Typically, this would be done while tracking down the source of an error, but it can just as easily be used to determine how something works.

Every time you copy and paste into Excel, you may find yourself in a situation where you are trying to figure out where a formula came from. This is simple enough when using formulas, but often it causes problems when using sheet functions. A common use of this would be when copying a report and trying to bring the sheets together or copying an invoice and trying to get the totals for each charge. The use of the "Trace Precedents" function will help you figure out what you did, and why. To figure out where a formula came from, first is make sure Excel has a formula on your sheet that you wish to trace. Next, click "Formula" from the top menu and click "Show All Formulas", select the cell(s) or range(s) containing your formula, then click "Trace Precedents".

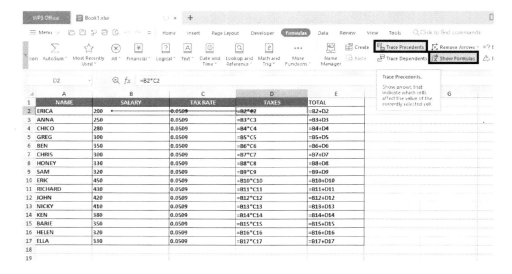

There are several different types of functions one can trace in Excel.

SUMPRODUCT

The most basic function that many people use is SUMPRODUCT(). This simply returns a result based on the values you input into it. For example, we could have a cell that says something like this: 1+2, 3+7 and 9+8. We could take these numbers and put them into SUMPRODUCT and get the result 30.

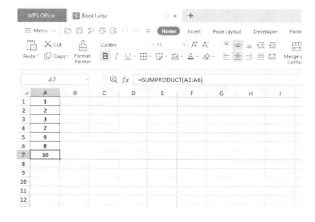

The next type of function we will look at is one that takes information from more than one cell. For example, if I want to take 6 different numbers, multiply them all together and then divide by 4, it will look like this: =SUMPRODUCT(A1*A2*A3*A4*A5*A6/4). This type of formula is most frequently used for an array multiplier for products such as sales figures, inventory, etc.

The last type of function that we will look at is a function that takes information from a cell and returns something based on a formula. For example, if we had a value in one cell, and wanted to find its square root, it would look like this: =SQRT(C2).

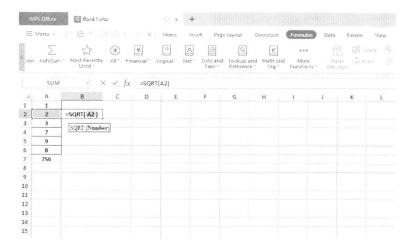

A lot of people like this type of formula because it is easier to write and still just as efficient.

When writing formulas in Excel, there are a lot of functions one can use. The main purpose of this book is to explain many different functions that are available in Excel and how they work.

Chapter 19.   DATA

Excel is an excellent tool for combining information from several different sources. However, before you can do this, you must import the data from the different sources into Excel first. You can either do this manually, or you can use the import function to automate the process.

IMPORTING DATA TEXT FILE

Excel allows you to import data from a variety of other types of files including CSV and TXT files. This chapter will show you how to import this type of data into your workbook as it goes step-by-step through the process.

In this example, we're importing data from a simple text file that contains only one row with one column of data. Select the cell you want to import data into.

1. To get started, click the Data tab on the Excel toolbar.

3. Choose Import Data tools section at the left of your screen. This option allows you to import data from a wide range of sources into Excel.

4. Next, select the text data format.

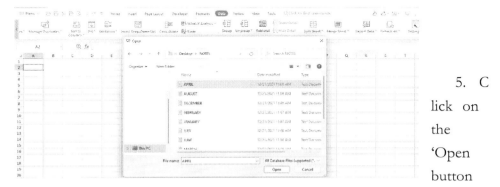

5. Click on the 'Open button to advance to the next page of the wizard and verify that you want to import all data from files, including any charts or graphs they contain, into a new table in your workbook.

This is very simple, but extremely powerful. If you need to use data from a database or website for your spreadsheet - just copy and paste it into the first cell of the first sheet and data will automatically be imported.

If you're using a lot of different types of data in your spreadsheet that don't look quite right against each other, then there's probably something wrong with how they're formatted. The issue is often caused by inconsistent column widths and thus their content not lining up as it should.

You can rectify that in seconds using the best feature of Numbers. It's called "AutoFormat" and this is what you'd use to fix it. Just select the cell or cells you want to format and then use the dropdown menu that appears to choose several different options. In nearly all cases this will result in everything lining up perfectly.

SORTING AND FILTERING

Sorting and Filtering are two of Excel's most useful features. They allow the user to quickly organize data into different categories, which makes it simpler for the user to find desired information and perform calculations.

Sorting is used to organize data into different categories, with each category sorted in ascending or descending order, depending on the options chosen. Users can also use sorting functions to combine two or more similar types of data into a single column and arrange them in order according to type. You can use the sorting function to sort your data by one of three different columns: name, date, or value. This can be done with a simple click of the button on top-right of your Excel window. The drop-down menu will allow you to choose which column to sort by. Example, if you want to sort your data by the column, "name," then simply click on the drop-down menu and choose "Name." If you want to sort your data by a date column, then just click on the drop-down menu and choose "Date" and so on.

Filtering is used when you have too many records for a spreadsheet and do not want them all displayed in one table. You can filter out rows that contain specific values in their headers without having to open them up and change them manually. For example, if you were an event planner, you could filter out all records that were not category specific which would save a lot of time when planning for the event. Filtering is also useful for eliminating unnecessary information from a spreadsheet helping it function more efficiently and quickly.

Excel offers two filtering options:

AUTO FILTER

AutoFilter is the default option and is easy to use, but it has few filtering options. The advantage of AutoFilter is that you can use drop-down menus to choose the items in the filtered list. AutoFilter is useful when you want to filter out rows or combine a group or two columns into one category.

ADVANCED FILTER

Advance Filter is the option that allows deeper filtering of rows or columns. Users must first determine how they want to filter the information and what columns to use for its filtering task. Advanced filters are very useful in many situations, such as when you want to filter out rows based on multiple criteria or perform calculations on the filtered data.

DATA VALIDATION

This is when you want Excel to check whether the data in your cells are in a certain range.

Validation criteria are composed with Whole number, Decimal, List, Date, Time and Text length.

Whole Number Criteria

For example, let's say that you want to make sure that the price of your product is no more than $400, you can add validation criteria based on this condition by selecting cells and clicking Data Validation on the Data Tab. Select the Whole Number option and set the Minimum amount and Maximum value.

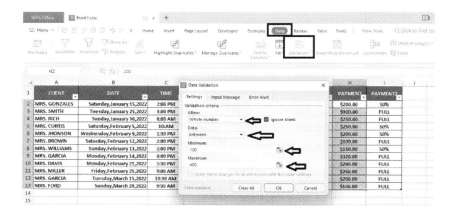

Input message

This is an optional message that can be displayed in a pop-up box when you click on the cell.

CLIENT	DATE	TIME	CHURCH	RECEPTION	BUNDLE	MOTIF	PAYMENT	PAYMENT2
MRS. GONZALES	Saturday, January 15, 2022	2:00 PM	ST. JOSEPH	USA		GREEN	$300.00	50%
MRS. SMITH	Tuesday, January 25, 2022	3:00 PM	ST. JOSEPH	UKRAINE	13	GRAY	AMOUNT	FULL
MRS. RICH	Sunday, January 30, 2022	8:00 AM	ST. JOSEPH	JAPAN	12	RED	AMOUNT	FULL
MRS. CURTIS	Saturday, February 5, 2022	10:AM	HOLY CROSS	CHINA	11	PURPLE	$250.00	50%
MRS. JHONSON	Wednesday, February 9, 2022	1:30 PM	HOLY CROSS	MEXICO	12	VIOLET	$200.00	50%
MRS. BROWN	Saturday, February 12, 2022	2:00 PM	STA. ANA	CANADA	11	YELLOW	$100.00	FULL
MRS. WILLIAMS	Sunday, February 13, 2022	3:00 PM	STA. ANA	HONGKONG	10	BLUE	$150.00	50%
MRS. GARCIA	Monday, February 14, 2022	4:00 PM	STA. ANA	DUBAI	9	MINT GREEN	$320.00	FULL
MRS. DAVIS	Monday, February 21, 2022	3:30 PM	REDEMPTORIST	PHILIPPINES	12	SKY BLUE	$280.00	FULL
MRS. MILLER	Friday, February 25, 2022	9:00 AM	REDEMPTORIST	AFRICA	12	ROYAL BLUE	$250.00	FULL
MRS. GARCIA	Tuesday, March 15, 2022	10:30 AM	ST. JOSEPH	AUSTRALIA	13	LAVANDER	$200.00	FULL
MRS. FORD	Sunday, March 20, 2022	9:30 AM	REDEMPTORIST	AMERICA	11	ORANGE	$100.00	FULL

Error Alert

This is another optional feature that will shows if the data you entered does not match the validation criteria. You can set the style, Title and the error message.

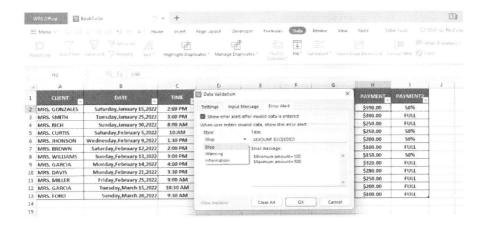

This is an example of how it looks like when the data in your cells are not in a certain range.

Decimal Criteria

If you have a product that has a decimal point, let's say your product is priced at $12.50. You can add validation criteria based on this condition by selecting cells and clicking Data Validation on the Data Tab. Select the Decimal option and set the Data to "Less Than" and set the Precision and set Minimum amount.

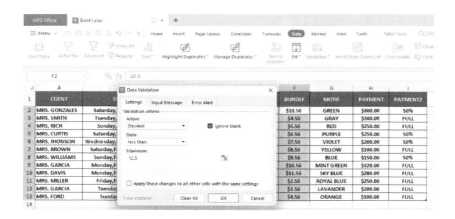

List Criteria

If you want to make sure that the data in your cells are from a certain drop down list, List criteria is the best option for you if you want to add validation on your cell based on a specific range of data.

Step 1: Create a new list for your source list.

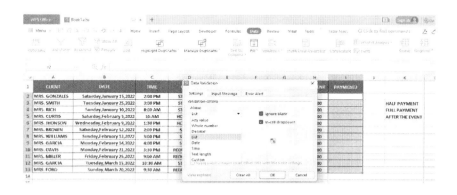

Step 2: Select cells that you want to add validation and go on a Data Tab and select List under Data Validation.

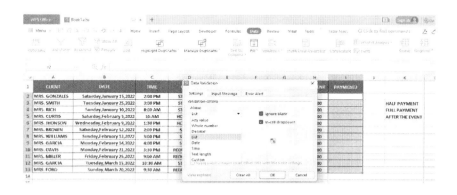

Step 3: Click the small square on the right side of the tab to get the list of your source.

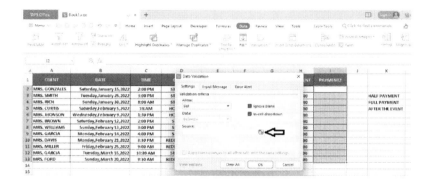

Step 4: Select the list of your source.

Step 5: Now, click OK to see the result. (Do not forget to delete your source list after setting up the validation)

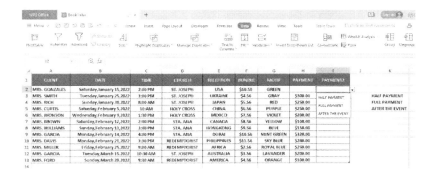

Date Criteria

If you have a schedule that requires a certain date, let's say the event will get expired after it reaches its target date. This is the perfect time to add validation on your cell based on the date by selecting cells and clicking Data Validation on the Data Tab. Select the Date option and input your date in a drop down box.

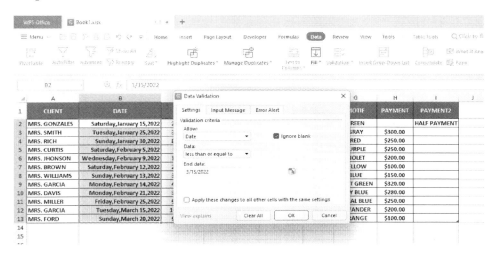

Let's assume the target date will be on March 14, 2022. Set the end date on March 15, 2022.

Notice the date on cell B13 (March 20, 2022), and when you click "Ok" you will then notice the red color on the cell.

CLIENT	DATE	TIME	CHURCH	RECEPTION	BUNDLE	MOTIF	PAYMENT	PAYMENT2
MRS. GONZALES	Saturday, January 15, 2022	2:00 PM	ST. JOSEPH	USA	$10.50	GREEN		HALF PAYMEN
MRS. SMITH	Tuesday, January 25, 2022	3:00 PM	ST. JOSEPH	UKRAINE	$4.56	GRAY	$300.00	
MRS. RICH	Sunday, January 30, 2022	8:00 AM	ST. JOSEPH	JAPAN	$5.56	RED	$250.00	
MRS. CURTIS	Saturday, February 5, 2022	10:AM	HOLY CROSS	CHINA	$6.56	PURPLE	$250.00	
MRS. JHONSON	Wednesday, February 9, 2022	1:30 PM	HOLY CROSS	MEXICO	$7.56	VIOLET	$200.00	
MRS. BROWN	Saturday, February 12, 2022	2:00 PM	STA. ANA	CANADA	$8.56	YELLOW	$100.00	
MRS. WILLIAMS	Sunday, February 13, 2022	3:00 PM	STA. ANA	HONGKONG	$9.56	BLUE	$150.00	
MRS. GARCIA	Monday, February 14, 2022	4:00 PM	STA. ANA	DUBAI	$10.56	MINT GREEN	$320.00	
MRS. DAVIS	Monday, February 21, 2022	3:30 PM	REDEMPTORIST	PHILIPPINES	$11.56	SKY BLUE	$280.00	
MRS. MILLER	Friday, February 25, 2022	9:00 AM	REDEMPTORIST	AFRICA	$2.56	ROYAL BLUE	$250.00	
MRS. GARCIA	Tuesday, March 15, 2022	10:30 AM	ST. JOSEPH	AUSTRALIA	$3.56	LAVANDER	$200.00	
MRS. FORD	Sunday, March 20, 2022	9:30 AM	REDEMPTORIST	AMERICA	$4.56	ORANGE	$100.00	

This means that the cell is not valid for any date that is after the inputted date.

To check this error, simply click the drop down tab and select edit formula the press OK.

This means that the cell is not valid for any date that is after the inputted date.

Time Criteria

An hour's difference can cause a lot of confusion. To prevent that, you can use a Time Criteria which will give you specific times. To set up this kind of validation, select cells and click Data Validation from the Data Tab. Select the Time option and input the time in the pop up box.

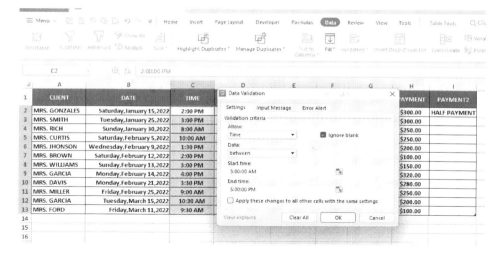

Text Length

If you have a product that has several words in its name, this will be a great way to ensure it can only contain specific characters. Find the cell where you want to use the validation. Select Data Validation on the Data Tab and click Text Length.

Now you can see that it is only allowed to have less than 10 characters in a cell.

If you enter more than 10 characters, you will get an error message.

	A	B	C	D	E	F	G	H	I
1	CLIENT	DATE	TIME	CHURCH	RECEPTION	BUNDLE	MOTIF	PAYMENT	PAYMENT2
2	MRS. GONZALES	Saturday, January 15, 2022	2:00 PM	ST. JOSEPH	USA	$10.50	GREEN	$300.00	HALF PAYMENT
3	MRS. SMITH	Tuesday, January 25, 2022	3:00 PM	ST. JOSEPH	UKRAINE	$4.56	GRAY	$300.00	FULL PAYMENT
4	MRS. RICH	Sunday, January 30, 2022	8:00 AM	ST. JOSEPH	JAPAN	$5.56	RED	$250.00	
5	MRS. CURTIS	Saturday, February 5, 2022	10:00 AM	HOLY CROSS	CHINA	$6.56	PURPLE	$250.00	
6	MRS. JHONSON	Wednesday, February 9, 2022	1:30 PM	HOLY CROSS	MEXICO	$7.56	VIOLET	$200.00	
7	MRS. BROWN	Saturday, February 12, 2022	2:00 PM	STA. ANA	CANADA	$8.56	YELLOW	$100.00	
8	MRS. WILLIAMS	Sunday, February 13, 2022	3:00 PM	STA. ANA	HONGKONG	$9.56	BLUE	$150.00	
9	MRS. GARCIA	Monday, February 14, 2022	4:00 PM	STA. ANA	DUBAI	$10.56	MINT GREEN	$320.00	
10	MRS. DAVIS	Monday, February 21, 2022	3:30 PM	REDEMPTORIST	PHILIPPINES	$11.56	Characters		
11	MRS. MILLER	Friday, February 25, 2022	9:00 AM	REDEMPTORIST	AFRICA	$2.56	Less than 10		
12	MRS. GARCIA	Tuesday, March 15, 2022	10:30 AM	ST. JOSEPH	AUSTRALIA	$3.56	Press [Enter] again to confirm		
13	MRS. FORD	Friday, March 11, 2022	9:30 AM	REDEMPTORIST	AMERICA	$4.56			
14									

To enter a word in cell B14, double-click on the red colored cell and type in your word and click Enter. You will then notice that the red color changes back to black. This means that your entry is valid now.

	A	B	C	D	E	F	G	H	I
1	CLIENT	DATE	TIME	CHURCH	RECEPTION	BUNDLE	MOTIF	PAYMENT	PAYMENT2
2	MRS. GONZALES	Saturday, January 15, 2022	2:00 PM	ST. JOSEPH	USA	$10.50	GREEN	$300.00	HALF PAYMENT
3	MRS. SMITH	Tuesday, January 25, 2022	3:00 PM	ST. JOSEPH	UKRAINE	$4.56	GRAY	$300.00	FULL PAYMENT
4	MRS. RICH	Sunday, January 30, 2022	8:00 AM	ST. JOSEPH	JAPAN	$5.56	RED	$250.00	
5	MRS. CURTIS	Saturday, February 5, 2022	10:00 AM	HOLY CROSS	CHINA	$6.56	PURPLE	$250.00	
6	MRS. JHONSON	Wednesday, February 9, 2022	1:30 PM	HOLY CROSS	MEXICO	$7.56	VIOLET	$200.00	
7	MRS. BROWN	Saturday, February 12, 2022	2:00 PM	STA. ANA	CANADA	$8.56	YELLOW	$100.00	
8	MRS. WILLIAMS	Sunday, February 13, 2022	3:00 PM	STA. ANA	HONGKONG	$9.56	BLUE	$150.00	
9	MRS. GARCIA	Monday, February 14, 2022	4:00 PM	STA. ANA	DUBAI	$10.56	MINTGREEN	$320.00	
10	MRS. DAVIS	Monday, February 21, 2022	3:30 PM	REDEMPTORIST	PHILIPPINES	$11.56	SKY BLUE	$280.00	
11	MRS. MILLER	Friday, February 25, 2022	9:00 AM	REDEMPTORIST	AFRICA	$2.56	ROYALBLUE	$250.00	
12	MRS. GARCIA	Tuesday, March 15, 2022	10:30 AM	ST. JOSEPH	AUSTRALIA	$3.56	LAVANDER	$200.00	
13	MRS. FORD	Friday, March 11, 2022	9:30 AM	REDEMPTORIST	AMERICA	$4.56	ORANGE	$100.00	
14									

Data validation is vital for your spreadsheets so that you can prevent errors from happening in your workbook. When entering the data in a worksheet you should make sure that the data is correct to prevent errors. This is how Data Validation works in excel.

REMOVE DUPLICATES

If you want to be 100% sure that what you have entered is a unique record, then it's better to remove duplicates before proceeding and using the value in excel. Creating a list of duplicate entries in the data entry screen will not do anything. It will only waste your time.

First is copy and paste your list to keep the original set. Now, click the HIGHLIGHT DUPLICATE in toolbar and select "REMOVE DUPLICATE".

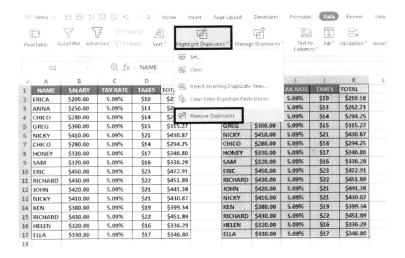

Now, click the HIGHLIGHT DUPLICATE in toolbar and select "REMOVE DUPLICATE".

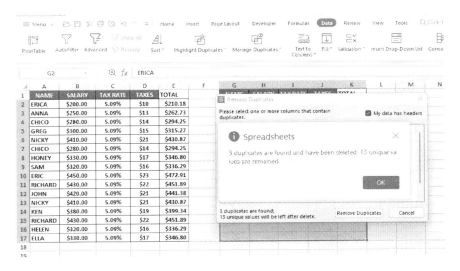

Now, check for duplicates in the list to find which one is the same as what you are looking for.

And that is how the list of duplicate records is removed.

Chapter 20.   CODING

VB macros are helpful in Excel. The VB Editor has a wealth of built-in and add-in commands that can help with various tasks. Macros can generate custom reports, automate repetitive actions, and even create new functions. It has been in the system for a long time, and it is such an effective tool for programming that most people are not even aware of its existence. This chapter will provide you with information about what VBA does and how to do it. When you have the basics down, you can decide whether this meets your needs or if there are better tools out there. Either way, it will give you a new way to think about developing your spreadsheets.

There are three versions of VBA included in Microsoft Office, which can each be accessed via their respective menus. When you access these menus, it should say "Developer's Tools" or something similar. The three options are Visual Basic, Visual Basic for Applications (VBA), and VBScript. They are each different and understand specific commands differently. For example, in Visual Basic, you can use the MsgBox function without quotes, but in VBA, you must have quotes around it. VBScript will complain if you do not include them. It is essential to know which language you need to use and be consistent with that language throughout your macro, or it will not work correctly. After you access the menu, the first option is to create a new project. This option is for all the VB languages. For ease of use, we will focus on VBA. Selecting this option will open Microsoft's Visual Basic Editor and create a new project with a default module. The module is the container that holds the code, which can be just one function or hundreds of lines of code. To write code in VBA, you must enter it into the module to make it active. This is done by selecting on the FILE menu and then selecting NEW and typing in the name of your module (no spaces). Once you enter the code, all your other commands will be available. To run a macro or function, you must click on VIEW and select either EDIT or TOOLS. When you use the TOOLS option, it will open a window with all available tools. The easiest to use is the VBE, which contains all the commands from the Visual Basic Editor. It will run as a background process.

The other options are for analyzing and debugging code. There are several ways to debug VBA code. The easiest is to click on DEBUG and SELECT TRACE TOOLS, which will bring up a window that allows you to select specific commands for your debugging needs. You can also use the SCREEN command to verify the output from your code. To view the VBA code itself, click on FILE > Open and select the module containing your code. It will open in the VBE, allowing you to view the code, and it will work without the need for the DEBUG command.

The biggest problem most people have with VBA is not understanding what it does to their spreadsheet. It will be complicated to decipher the differences between VBA and a free version of Excel. Many spreadsheets have code, but you cannot tell what it does or how it is structured. Even if you know the language, it can be intimidating to change something already been created. It will be necessary to take notes from time to time as you learn new commands that may be useful. You will find that some commands are very similar to their plain English counterparts but often have minor variations.

Chapter 21. MACROS IN MICROSOFT EXCEL AND REMINDERS

A macro is a recording of how you need to act, like, for example, calculating some things. Using macros in Microsoft Excel will help you open and close your workbook quickly. You can also use them to remember important tasks like putting something in the "to-do" list or scheduling a meeting. You can also use macros to automate repetitive tasks. You don't have to write your action steps down by hand anymore since they are recorded in a macro.

A macro can be used to:

1. Calculate or modify a series of numbers, values, or text automatically.
2. Display specific information in a cell automatically.
3. Repeat a set of instructions or actions periodically.
4. Edit the contents of an entire workbook at one time by running a single command.

The macros created can also remind you of the tasks you have to do at the beginning of a week or month. For example, you will create a macro that will send you an email each time you open a specific workbook so that when it is ready, you will know precisely when it was created. This way, if something goes wrong or something else happens in the future, there won't be confusion over what action was taken and when. You can also use macros to help you with repetitive tasks that you have to do daily. This can be done by selecting some tasks and recording them as macros. For example, if you like to print a headings page whenever you start working on a project, you can record the steps needed to do this using the macro recorder. Then all you will have to remember is to click "Apply" on your keyboard instead of having to re-record all the steps each time you need it.

To record and playback macros in Microsoft Excel, you must enable the "Developer" option in Excel's menu bar and then click the Developer tab. There you will see the Macro dialog box.

You will be prompted if you want to record your actions or just open the Visual Basic Editor when you do that. If you choose to record your steps, Excel will start recording everything that happens on your screen. When you are done recording, you need to stop the recording by clicking the Stop Recording button in the Developer tab. If you choose instead to open the Visual Basic Editor, you will view your macro code and edit it if needed. Then, once your macro is ready, click "Record" in the Macro dialog box to turn it into a macro. This option allows you to store multiple macros in one place and run them one after another by selecting a particular sequence from a drop-down list.

Excel macros are powerful tools that allow you to automate repetitive tasks, but they can also be confusing. You may wonder what will happen in the case of an error or a computer crash. That is why you should consider using macros only if you know how to use them properly. For example, a great idea would be to create macros that print documents or workbooks in random order so that if something happens the next time someone opens them, you will still have a valid copy.

Another essential thing to remember is that macros are very easy to corrupt since they usually do not store any information about their previous executions. Therefore, only the most used macros should be recorded and stored in one place.

If you need to edit the macro, you can press Alt + F11 on your keyboard to open the Microsoft Visual Basic for Applications window. Then you can open your macro by going through Tools > Macro > Macros. Once it is opened, there will be a sheet with a recorded list of macros. You will then see the main code window where you can edit your macro code. The Visual Basic Code Editor will then show you a line of code. When you right-click it, there will be a list of the different commands in Excel and other programs that can be used on that line. Simply double-click the command or drag and drop it in your code window to insert one of them.

Click "Save" to save your macro before closing it. Microsoft Excel's macro recorder is a useful function that can help you do things much more quickly. However, recording macros can be risky if you don't know how to use them properly. If you would like to start recording your actions, make sure that you are aware of all the risks and check what kinds of actions will significantly impact your workbook should something go wrong.

You can also use Macros to remind yourself about the meeting with your boss, tasks that you need to do at work, or anything you must make sure you won't forget in the future. You can record a macro that will send an email to yourself each time you open a specific workbook so that when it is ready, you will know precisely when it was created.

It is essential to realize that Macros are not intended to enter data; this action should be done manually per company policy. The macro should be used to save time and energy by performing tasks that typically require the use of keyboard shortcuts instead of keeping track of where the mouse is located and repeatedly clicking keys.

ADVANTAGES OF MACRO IN EXCEL

Macros have many benefits, including:

1. They can make your work easier.
2. They can help you ensure that you don't forget any important task or deadline. You can choose to remind yourself of the tasks or deadlines by playing back the macro at a specific time or date, when your workbook is opened, or when "something" happens on your screen, like opening a particular file or clicking a button.
3. You can perform repetitive tasks that you have to do daily with macros.
4. They can be used to ensure that you will have the necessary information on hand when a project is assigned to you. This can prevent many headaches when the time comes for submitting the report or answering some questions in your group meetings.

DISADVANTAGES OF MACRO IN EXCEL

While macros are handy, there are also some disadvantages:

1. They may not always work depending on what version of Microsoft Excel you're using or if your macros have been corrupted.
2. They can be confusing when you first use them. It is essential to keep in mind that macros are not intended to create and edit your workbook directly.
3. It can be challenging to train new employees because they might not know the proper way to use macros, so it's a good idea for them to know macros before being trusted with the task of creating and editing macros.
4. Your company's security settings may not permit them. Also, they can be disabled by the company's antivirus program.
5. You need to learn the correct keystrokes to use macros efficiently.

Macros can be a valuable and time-saving feature in Microsoft Excel, but you need to ensure that you are using them correctly. While it may seem tempting to just record your actions and create a macro, this can be dangerous if you don't know what you're doing. Instead, choose an important task that you do daily, record the process of completing it with all the necessary steps, then use the macro each day when you need to complete it.

Another important thing to set in mind is not to send the same email to all your co-workers or clients if you want to explain something in a meeting before the actual meeting takes place. Instead, create a macro that will send a different email each time, depending on who you choose to send your message to. This way, you will easily make changes if something doesn't go as planned.

Chapter 22.   EXCEL SHORTCUTS AND TIPS

Are you new to Microsoft Excel? Confusing menus and formatting tips can make a spreadsheet seem more daunting than it is. Luckily, there are plenty of shortcuts that you should know before getting started on your spreadsheet. These tips are intentional to help you save time and increase productivity while looking great in the process. Whatever the case may be, beginners will be glad to have these handy shortcuts at their fingertips!

KEYBOARD SHORTCUTS

The following are some of the most used shortcuts to save time and increase productivity:

CTRL + C: Copy the item immediately to the right

CTRL + V: Paste the item that was copied to the right

CTRL + Z: Undo last action

ALT + SHIFT + . : Strikethrough (This will delete the cell contents of the cells selected.)

Can be used with a letter to highlight all cells beginning with that letter.

CTRL + I: Change the font formatting of the entire row or column.

ALT + SHIFT + O: Creates a chart from data in a selected range.

ALT+F11: Shows the Microsoft Visual Basic Editor window, where you can access all VBA code for your workbook.

That's a lot of shortcuts, but it's worth remembering them-- especially when you're working with spreadsheets. Once you start applying these shortcuts, you'll wonder how you ever got by without them!

FORMATTING TIPS

In addition to the keyboard shortcuts listed above, there are also dozens of different formatting shortcuts that can be used to improve your documents. These tips will help you not only produce legible worksheets and documents, but also save time as well.

1. The little curved arrow on the Home key can be used to quickly jump from one cell to another.

2. When you're entering a value, it's usually a good idea to enter it in one cell and then press SHIFT to put it into all adjacent cells. This will give you an exact value instead of a fraction of each adjoining cell.

3. When using the formula bar in Excel, there are countless shortcuts that can be used to create formulas faster. There are quick key combinations that can be used to create formulas that display on the right side of the formula bar automatically.

4. If you're typing a lot of words that are analogous, you will find it quicker to use Excel's "AutoComplete" feature than to type it out yourself. This feature detects the most used words in your document and fills them in for you. It doesn't work on all problematic words like "and" but it does work well with most words, such as the word "city".

5. If you're working with a large spreadsheet that has many columns, but you only want to see the column that you're currently typing in, make sure to change your view. You can apply so by pressing the "Ctrl" button and selecting "View." Under this tab, there will be a box with three different view options: View as single column, View as double columns, and View as gridlines on. Select "View as single column" and that column will be the only one you see on your screen.

6. If you are dealing with a lot of columns, which means you have a lot of information to look at, you can use the "Go To Second Column" feature in Excel. This function will let you instantly go to the second column on the worksheet. To do this, press SHIFT+F9, which jumps directly to the second column and stays there until released.

7. It's a good idea to use plenty of white space in your spreadsheet. This makes it easier for people to read the information that you've included and gives the impression that there is more content than there actually is. It also makes it easier to find important information briefly.

8. Use a separate ink pen when writing in your spreadsheet. You can use different-colored ink to create your own color coding system. This is of great usefulness if you're dealing with a very large document or if you're using several different fonts in your documents and you want to differentiate between them visually.

9. If you're working with graphics, don't forget to use "Alignment" in the "Format menu." You can also use "Line Spacing" as well. This can greatly improve the look of your graphics in a spreadsheet.

10. If you're using columns, you'll find that they are easy to change and manipulate. You can do this by using the "Home" key and then selecting the right-hand arrow beside it. This will allow you to quickly change your entire column's orientation without breaking a sweat.

11. You can change the font in Excel quite easily. Just press "F11" to bring up the "Font" menu and then choose a different font. This is very useful if you're working with only one type of font in your document.

12. If you have trouble with names that are very long, it's a good idea to use a label feature to help you flesh out your spreadsheet. This

feature can split up names into individual labels and make it easier to read through your document after it's been completed.

13. If you're working with very large documents, you might notice that your document is taking longer to sort than normal. This can be due to the amount of data being entered. Try using the "Sort" function in Excel.

14. When sorting "Columns" (or "Rows") select a column or row and then hit "Tab," and it will sort that area first. If the desired column or row does not appear in the drop-down menu, it is probably because you haven't selected the entire column or row yet.

15. You can use your arrow keys to navigate a worksheet much faster than using the mouse.

16. Don't forget to color-code your spreadsheets! You can do this by using many different techniques, such as: Using a different font color, using a unique background color, or using both at the same time!

17. If you want to merge your cells, you can use the "Home" button. Pressing "Ctrl" and the left-hand button will merge the cells by rows and pressing "Shift" and the right-hand button will merge them by columns.

18. If you're working on a spreadsheet with a lot of data in it, use the feature that allows you to filter data out of your document by using different criteria. This can easily be done by going to the top of your spreadsheet and clicking on "Data. " From there, click on "Filter" and then you can select which criteria you want to filter out.

19. You can easily hide columns or rows in a spreadsheet by going to the top of your document, clicking on the "View" tab, and selecting either "Hide Columns" or "Hide Rows."

20. You can right-click on any of your cells and find a long list of options that will do it simpler for you to format your document. Just be careful about what you pick!

21. If you're typing in an area that's very large, it's a good idea to make the font size of your text much smaller. This way, you can fit more data on a single page without having to scroll as much.

TOOLS SHORTCUTS

If you have time, the best thing to do is go through all the key combinations and enter them all in your keyboard. The shortcuts allow you to access Excel faster than if you just went through all the steps in this guide step by step.

1. If you want to open Excel from Word, select "Home" and then "Start" and then click on "Excel." This will bring up a new document that has been created as an Excel workbook.

2. If you don't have time to use all the shortcuts in this guide, at least try to use the ones that are used in the "File" menu. You can access this by pressing "Ctrl" and "F11." Some of the important file commands include Save as, Save, Save As Another File, New Workbook/File, Open Workbook/File, Close Workbook/File, Print Preview, and Exit.

3. If you want to create a new workbook, select "New" and click on "Workbook."

4. Click on the "File" option on your toolbar and then click on "Open" to open your workbook. This will show up a dialog box that lets you select which Excel file you want to open.

5. Click on the "File" option from your toolbar and then click on "Open" to open another Excel document that was saved in the same folder as your original one.

6. You can also access the options in this dialog box by pressing "Ctrl" and "O."

7. If you want to save your file as a different file type, select "Save As" and then take the format that you want it to be.

8. If you're working on a newer version of Excel, click on "Options" in the top right corner of your screen and then press on "Save." When you do this, it will bring up a dialog box that lets you control where your documents are saved and how they are saved.

9. If you want to access your file directly from the open program menu, press "Alt" and click on the "File" option along the top of your screen.

10. If you want to close an Excel document without having to save it first, simply press "Ctrl" and "F4." This will prompt you to save it before closing it, even if you have unsaved changes.

11. If you want to close Excel without being prompted to save documents, press "F12" and then click on the "Yes" button.

12. If you want to print your document on a different printer than your default one, be sure to check out the Print Shortcuts section of this guide!

13. To add a file extension to an Excel document that already exists, select "File" and click on "Info." Then click on the "Save" tab and click on the box next to "Add To File Name. "

14. When you're viewing a file, you can rename it by pressing "F2" and then typing in the new name of your file.

15. If you want to print your spreadsheet, click on "File" and click on "Print." Then click on the printer that you want to print from and select your desired print options.

16. If you want to know what version of Excel you're using, press "Ctrl" and "Q" and then click on "About." This will show up a dialog box that shows you exactly what version it is.

17. If you want to know how much space your workbook takes up on your computer, press "Ctrl" and "Q." Then, click on the "Size" tab near the top of the screen and it will tell you how much space it's taking up in megabytes.

18. If you want to zoom in or out of your spreadsheet, hold down the "Ctrl" key and click on the "+" or "- " signs found on your top toolbar.

19. To access your most recently used files, click on "File" and then click on "Open Recent." This will show up a dialog box that shows you all the files that you've opened recently.

20. If you want to copy the entire row that your cursor is currently in, press "Alt" and then press "down arrow." If you want to copy all the cells that are directly above your cursor, press "Alt" and then press "up arrow."

21. If you want to cut the entire row that your cursor is currently in, press "Ctrl" and then click on the "X" button. If you want to cut all the cells that are directly above your cursor, hold down "Ctrl" and click on the box at the top of your screen.

22. If you want to move the entire row that your cursor is in, simply click on the empty space on the left side of your screen and drag it over to where you want it. If you want to move all the cells that are directly above your cursor, click on the empty space at the top of your screen and drag it over to where you want it.

These tips are just a few of the things that you can do with Excel. There are tons of shortcuts and features that you can use to make your work easier, faster and smoother. Just remember to take it slow when you're first attempting to learn Excel. You can always come back and learn later what the shortcuts are.

Chapter 23.   FAQS

The Microsoft excel FAQs are a helpful guide that addresses some of the most common questions and frequently asked problems about this application. It is an easy-to-read document that you can always keep on hand when you have questions about what excel does or how to do specific tasks.

Gain insight into how Microsoft excel works, determine which formulas are used most often, and learn what the various apps do in this article. This document will provide an excellent resource for users looking for information on how to use or make calculations with Excel. It is also a valuable way for beginners to learn what excel does and how you can start using the app.

Operate this guide as a source of information that will help you to understand how to use the various features of Microsoft excel.

Frequently Asked Questions about Microsoft Excel

Q. How does Microsoft excel work?

A. Microsoft excel is a spreadsheet application that can be used for all tasks. It offers a user-friendly way to create spreadsheets that contain data and information. You can organize the data into rows and columns and save the file as an Excel spreadsheet.

Q. How do I open the program?

A. Launch the Microsoft excel program by double-clicking on its icon on your desktop or in your programs list.

Q. What types of tasks can I perform with Microsoft excel?

A. The Microsoft excel program can be used for an assortment of tasks. These include setting up a household budget, creating a recipe book, managing finances, and organizing your life in general. In addition to these practical uses, you can use it to create spreadsheets for things like analysis or college budgets and schedules.

Q. Can I create financial spreadsheets with Microsoft excel?

A. Yes, you can also use the Microsoft Excel program to create financial spreadsheets. These spreadsheets can include loan payments, savings plans, and budgets.

Q. What does Excel do?

A. Microsoft excel is a spreadsheet application that allows you to organize and display data in rows and columns. Using this program, many tasks can be completed, including setting up a household budget or recipe book, managing finances, creating personal documents, and editing photos. The program can be used for just about any type of task that you need to be done.

Q. How do I create a spreadsheet?

A. To create a spreadsheet, begin with the menu options, which can be accessed by clicking on the top menu bar and selecting "File" at the top of the menu. The "File" option is located on the left side of this bar. From this location, click on "New" then select "Spreadsheet." This will launch the blank spreadsheet and allow you to start adding data and information.

Q. How do I format cells?

A. Formatting cell is one way to make your spreadsheets more eye-catching and easier to understand. There are several ways to format cells, including changing the color, font style, or alignment of the text. To apply this, choose the cell or range of cells that you would like to change, then click on "Home" from the menu bar at the top of your screen. From here, select the options that you would like to apply.

Q. How do I create a chart in Excel?

A. To create a chart, you must first open the spreadsheet that contains your data and information. From here, select the "Insert" option from the menu bar at the top of your screen, then click on "Chart." This will show a new pop-up window where you can select different types of graphs to use. Once you have chosen a chart type, click on "OK," and you will be prompted to enter additional details such as labels and titles.

Q. How do I save my worksheet?

A. Saving your work is an essential part of using the Microsoft Excel program. You can either choose to save your work as you are creating it or save it later. Keeping it as you create it will allow you to resume your work if you need to leave or close the program. You can also set multiple versions of the same file, which is useful should you need to go back and set changes or corrections to your original work.

Q. How do I use the autosum feature?

A. To use the autosum feature of Microsoft Excel, select the cells you would like to sum and then click on "Data" from the menu bar. From here, select "AutoSum," which is located at the bottom of the drop-down menu. This will instinctively add all your selected cells and automatically fill in any blank spaces with zeroes.

Q. What does autofill do?

A. Autofill is a handy tool that can help to save time when using Microsoft excel. Using autofill is one way to organize and track multiple tasks that you need to complete, such as paying bills and planning out your finances.

Q. How do I remove rows, columns, or text?

A. There are a range of ways to remove rows, columns, or text within a spreadsheet. To delete a row, click on the "Home" button on your menu and select "Delete." This will take you back to the previous screen, where you can choose which cells you would like to delete. To delete text, select the cell containing the text you would like to remove and click on "Home" again, then choose "Delete." To delete a column, select the column and click on "Home," then select "Delete."

Q. How do I calculate percentages in Excel?

A. Calculating percentages in Microsoft excel is a great way to display information visually and save time when calculating totals. There are range ways that you can complete this task, including using the percentage key on your keyboard or using formulas and functions.

Q. How do I find an average in Excel?

A. Finding averages in Microsoft excel is a great way to compare different numbers and find out how they stack up against your data. There are several ways to complete this task, including using the "Sum" formula, using the "Average" function, or using autofill.

Q. What do Paste Values do?

A. Paste values are a function that automatically updates the rest of the spreadsheet based on the information that you pasted. This is helpful if you use an Excel database or Google doc to update several different spreadsheets at once.

Q. How do I create a row number?

A. Creating row numbers in Microsoft excel is easy because it can be done simply by clicking on a cell and selecting "Row and Column" from the drop-down menu. From here, choose "Insert Row Number." This will automatically add a number based on the total number of rows in your spreadsheet.

Q. How do I create a column number?

A. Creating column numbers in Microsoft excel is easy because it can be done simply by clicking on a cell and selecting "Columns" from the drop-down menu. From here, choose "Insert Column." This will automatically add numbers based on the total number of columns in your spreadsheet.

Q. How do I use conditional formatting?

A. Using conditional formatting to color-code data is a great way to track and organize information. This is especially valuable when working on multiple spreadsheets at once, such as managing your finances, tracking your latest purchases, or creating a pie chart for each month.

Q. How do I insert a hyperlink?

A. Inserting hyperlinks in Microsoft excel is quick and easy when using the "Hyperlink" function located on the "Insert" option at the upper of your screen. Simply enter the link that you would like to use and then click on "Hyperlink."

Q. How do I sort a column?

A. Sorting in Microsoft excel is a great way to organize and track information. When sorting a column, simply click on the "Home" button on your menu bar and click on "Sort." From here, select what type of sorting you would like to complete, such as alphabetically or numerically.

Q. How do I insert pictures to my spreadsheets?

A. Adding pictures to Microsoft excel spreadsheets is quick and easy. Just click on "Insert" in the menu bar at the top of your screen, then select "Picture." This will launch a new window that you can use to upload your picture from your favorite images hosting sites, such as Picasa or Flickr.

Q. How do I change font colors in Excel?

A. Changing colors in Microsoft excel is a great way to emphasize different parts of your spreadsheet because of its versatility. You can choose a different font, outline text using bold, or set the background color. To change the font color, simply click on "Home" on your menu bar, select "Font," and select an option. If you want to create the text bolder, simply right-click on the cell and select "Bold." If you're going to set the background color, click on the "Page Layout" option on your menu bar, then choose "Background."

Q. Why do I make a graph?

A. Graphs in Microsoft excel are a great way to compare different numbers or categories. You can use graphs to compare sales over time, create pie charts or line charts and create scatterplots that show trends over time.

Q. What is an XML file, and how do I open one?

A. An XML file is a text file that includes data in a structured format. This is helpful for compatibility between different computer applications. To open an XML file, click on "Open" in the menu bar and select "Choose Windows." Then simply browse your computer until you find the XML file you would like to open.

Q. How do I send an Excel email?

A. Sending emails with Microsoft excel is a great way to stay organized and share your information with others easily. All you need are your contacts and the link to download your spreadsheet. They can then download any information they need, such as recent purchases or employee paychecks.

Q. What is a pivot table?

A. Pivot tables are great for displaying data on two different sheets of a spreadsheet at once, so making one will help you keep track of how much money you spend each month and how much interest you paid on your bills.

Q. How do I create a chart with multiple series?

A. Creating multi-series graphs in Microsoft Excel is very easy and can be done by clicking on "Insert" on the option bar and then selecting "Chart." From here, you will want to use the drop-down menu and select "Pie Series." This will create a new series that you can use to create your graph.

Q. What does the error saying "You cannot delegate access to worksheet 'insert sheet name' because it is not a trusted source"?

A. This error shows up when someone tries to access a spreadsheet you have shared with them through an app such as Google docs. To fix this error, simply click on "File" then "Info." Under the Protection tab, select "Trusted Sources" and choose anyone you want to be able to access your spreadsheets.

Q. What is the great way to collaborate with other people on a spreadsheet?

A. When trying to collaborate on a spreadsheet, it is helpful to use Microsoft excel' s "Shared with me" option. This will let you or your coworkers to open the same spreadsheet and add information. This is an excellent way for people to track their expenses.

Q. What does the error saying "This workbook contains links to other files that are stored on your computer so you can use them in this workbook. The files are automatically updated when you open this file, but if the file has been moved or renamed on your computer, clicking one of these links won't update the link correctly"?

A. This error shows up when an invalid link is used in the spreadsheet, like when someone goes to a different location on their computer and opens an older version of the same workbook. To fix this error, simply right-click on the cell that contains the link and select "Delete Link."

Q. Can I send a spreadsheet as an attachment?

A. Sending a spreadsheet as an attachment is very useful if you are collaborating with coworkers or partners that you do not work with all the time. You can quickly send them the information they need to see, such as your weekly or monthly expenses.

Q. What does the error saying "This workbook is locked. If you need to update it, unlock it and then save it again"?

A. This error shows up when someone tries to open an excel file that is locked by someone else using the same computer. Simply unlock the spreadsheet by clicking on "File" and "Info," then select the Protection tab to fix this error.

Q. How do I change my background color?

A. The background color is a great way to customize and brand your spreadsheet or document, so it stands out from others. Click on " Home " to change the background color, click on "Home" then select "Background." Select a new color in the drop-down menu.

Q. How do I get rid of a comment?

A. Click on the "Comments" tab toward the top of your screen. Then select "Delete Comment" and click on the cell that contains the comment you want to get rid of.

Q. How do I make my spreadsheet printable?

A. This is a great way to keep track of important documents and stay organized. To make your spreadsheet printable, click on "Page Layout" in the menu bar, then select "Page Setup." Then under margins, select "None" on both sides.

Q. What does the error saying "Cannot open file c:\list1.xls from the location C:\Users\Teddi Klein\Documents\Excel\My Workbooks" mean?

A. This error shows up when Excel cannot open a file that has the same name as another file inside of your "Documents" folder. Simply delete the old excel file and rename it to fix this error.

Q. What are Microsoft Excel's features?

A. Microsoft Excel does not have a set feature list. It is designed to help users create different worksheets, lists, and graphs in a spreadsheet format that can easily be shared with other people or saved for future use. Users can have multiple views of their workbook from the main menu and can also save their workbooks so that they can be shared securely with others who may or may not have Excel installed on their devices

Q. What is compatibility?

A. Compatibility is an application's ability to run on different devices, operating systems, and software versions. Microsoft Excel is compatible with Windows 2002 and above, including Windows 10. Microsoft Excel also has a version for Mac OS X. Microsoft Excel can be used to create spreadsheets from any data source that's compatible with Excel's file format.

Q. What is a workbook?

A. A workbook is a file that's created by an Excel program. Each workbook contains one or more worksheets, which are sheets. The worksheet name shows up at the top of each sheet and can have lists, charts, and columns of data.

Q. What is a sheet?

A. A sheet is a single area within a workbook. It has cells, each with its cell address, but no other functionality beyond displaying data and running formulas (see below).

Q. What are timesheet templates?

A. Timesheets are templates used to track time spent on specific tasks and help you bill your clients correctly. Excel has different built-in timesheet templates, or you can create one (here is an excellent guide on creating your own).

Q. What is an Excel template?

A. Templates are files that provide a basic structure for your workbooks. Using a template as a beginning point for a new workbook can help you quickly create organized and professional-looking worksheets.

With the help of this FAQS, your queries about Microsoft excel are solved.

We hope this will be helpful for you and guide you to understand your software and master your skills to create promising projects.

CONCLUSION

Microsoft Excel is one of the most commonly-used applications in the world. You'll need to know your way around functions and formulas to use them efficiently and productively. It's used to present data in charts and tables, calculate automatically, and manage large volumes of data. Excel has countless features that you need to be familiar with. But it's also easy to use, and there is no need to have any prior experience. This means that anyone who knows how to work with a spreadsheet can learn how to use Microsoft Excel proficiently. The basics are handled in the first steps. You need to understand the standard and advanced functions to stay on task. The navigation and formatting options will help you create a data table that is appropriately formatted. You'll be able to make an effective chart with relative ease after flipping through the pages in this guide. When you have the basic knowledge of how Microsoft excel works, you can build on those skills and add creativity. These points will help you build skills for a lifetime. Not many people will regret the time spent learning how to master Microsoft excel. You can share your charts with the entire world. The possibilities of what you can do are numerous. Even if you don't plan to use excel every day, it's still worth your time to learn how it works beforehand. This will provide you with a good head start on creating your first spreadsheet or chart. Each new skill you learn will be easier to master Microsoft excel. You can develop your skills faster if you search for answers to specific problems. Keeping your skills sharp is easy once you know how to use Microsoft excel. You can find a solution to your questions with a few search terms and the web. This book is created to help you master Microsoft Excel and get answers to your questions. Reducing your learning curve increases the amount of work you can accomplish each day. Be sure that you're on the right track by reading those tips before pressing on with this guide. You'll acquire the skills you need more easily after studying this guide. If you improve your skills as outlined in this guide, it will benefit your life in many ways. If you're seeking for a great way to master the MS excel functions, look no further!

THE END

Made in the USA
Columbia, SC
01 April 2022

58378201R00117